THAI
SLOW COOKER
COOKBOOK

THAI SLOW COOKER COOKBOOK

Classic Thai Favorites
Made Simple

ROCKRIDGE
PRESS

Interior photographs © Wolfgang Schardt/StockFood, p. 2; Gräfe & Unzer Verlag/Grossmann.Schuerle/StockFood, p. 5; Natasha Breen/Shutterstock, p. 6; Michael Wissing/StockFood, p. 10; Jennifer Martine/StockFood, p. 20; Martin Dyrlov/StockFood, p. 34; Marie José Jarry/StockFood, p. 44; Sporrer/Skowronek/Stockfood, p. 60; Fotosearch RM/StockFood, p. 68; Tanya Zouev/Stockfood, p. 76; Sam Stowell/StockFood, p. 90; Valerie Janssen/StockFood, p. 102; Tanya Zouev/StockFood, p. 116; Harry Bischof/StockFood, p. 134. All other photos Shutterstock.com.

ISBN: Print 978-1-62315-596-4
eBook 978-1-62315-650-3

CONTENTS

INTRODUCTION

....

Thai cuisine is much more than the sum of its dishes. With it comes a rich food culture steeped in tradition passed down through generations. For centuries, putting a meal on the table as nourishing as it is aesthetically pleasing has been the daily mission of men and women throughout Thailand. Ancient Siam kings so loved their dishes that they devoted poetry to their food and sought out the finest chefs to cook for their royal courts. Cooking is a task handled with great pride and skill, with many recipes handed down from as far back as history can dictate. It is on the shoulders of this colorful culinary heritage that this book rests.

At the mention of Thai food, "spicy" may very likely be the first thought that comes to mind. But focusing solely on this aspect gives you an incomplete picture. While known for its fiery soups, salads, and curries, Thai food is really all about balance. Many of the most recognized Thai dishes rely on the rich sweetness of coconut milk to mask the intense heat of chiles, while others opt instead to mix salty and sour elements for a taste bud-popping combination. However presented, the complex balance of sweet, spicy, sour, and salty is what makes many of the cuisine's most popular dishes so distinctly Thai.

For years, Thai cuisine has seemed unachievable at home. Instead, its preparation was left to the confines of the growing Thai restaurant community found speckled throughout large and small cities worldwide. However, with the influx of Thai food exporters and greater access to more of its key ingredients, creating Thai food at home is no longer the mystifying task it was 20 years ago.

Today, many mainstream grocery stores stock the basic ingredients for a variety of Thai foods, giving you little need to travel elsewhere. Some harder to find ingredients, such as Thai vegetables, fresh turmeric, whole fishes, or lime leaves, may require a trip to a local Asian market or an online order. The growing demand for these products, inspired both by an increasing interest in healthy cuisine and a growing Thai expat community, has opened the door for you to prepare these nutritious dishes from the comfort of your own home.

If you are daunted by the various processes for cooking Thai food, don't be. This book dispels any myths regarding the complexity of cooking Thai food while introducing a modern approach to preparing Thai food the slow cooker way. Today's busy work schedules and family commitments can make getting a meal on the table every day a real challenge. That's why this book combines convenience and delicious eats, presenting a medley of slow cooker recipes as simple to prepare as they are flavorful to.

Authentic Thai food pays close attention to ingredient choice, but this doesn't mean that for a dish to be authentic, every element must be created from scratch. In this book, you have the choice of making curry pastes from scratch or purchasing ready-made varieties from the store. What is important, however, when creating authentic Thai foods is using fresh and appropriate ingredients following the Thai tradition. Therefore, using the slow cooker to make these Thai foods allows you to maintain authenticity without sacrificing convenience.

The mixture of traditional and modern Thai-fusion recipes presented in this book places the power to create delicious, healthy Thai food at your fingertips. By blending classic recipes with the modern slow cooker, you can enjoy the best of both worlds, and let your slow cooker do most of the work for you. Set it—just be sure not to forget it!—and a delicious meal will be awaiting your return home.

PART ONE

Thai Food, Meet Slow Cooker

1

EVERYDAY THAI COOKING

....

Pad thai and green curry are two of the most ubiquitous Thai foods, finding their way onto most Thai menus throughout the world. However, these two regional dishes are just a small snapshot of a highly diverse cuisine.

Before the advent of modern transportation, many regions of Thailand were shrouded by thick forest and mountains, making them inaccessible to those outside the immediate area, even close neighbors. Because of this, regional cuisine was based largely on the foods directly available in one's own community. Vast differences in growing conditions, as well as vegetable and protein availability, led to different styles of cuisine varying widely from one far-flung region of the country to another.

In the fourteenth century, Thailand became a unified nation. As travel throughout the country became more viable over the next several centuries, new ingredients were introduced to different regions, and the once solid lines between regional variations became increasingly skewed. Today, Thai food is divided into four regions, while even finer distinctions remain among these few. From house to house, village to village, and city to city, countless variations exist in preparation style, ingredients, and recipes, all of which contribute to the unique nature of Thai cuisine.

In northern Thailand, an area characterized by mountains, rivers, and dense forests, the Lao, Burmese, Hmong, Karen, and other ethnicities have brought their influences to the cuisine known for grilled meats and fiery hot sausages. Northeastern Thailand, also called the Issan region, is an area prone to drought, intense heat, and monsoons. Unsurprisingly, these conditions lead to infertile soil, so this cuisine makes use of limited staples in multiple ways to create a treasure trove of dishes. Here, fermented fish is widely used for flavoring, as is the biting heat of small, dried red chiles. In both northern and Issan cuisine, sticky rice, or glutinous rice, is the accompaniment of choice.

Central Thailand is an area lush with fertile soil and access to the Gulf of Thailand. The plentiful fresh fish, crab, shrimp, and mollusks available make their way regularly to the plate. A wide variety of fruits and vegetables show up, as well, both cooked and raw, in countless dishes. The balance of salty, sweet, and tart flavors is a mainstay in central Thai cuisine, where palm sugar, lime, tamarind, coconut cream, and shrimp paste are in abundance. This is in contrast to further south, where you can find some of the country's spiciest cuisine. A large Muslim population along the winding coastline enjoys ample seafood, fruits, and coconuts, as well as the regional specialty, goat. As an accompaniment to central and southern Thai cuisine, jasmine rice is served, rather than the sticky rice seen in Northern and Issan cuisine.

Many of the most iconic dishes of Thailand, such as fried noodles and coconut-based curries, hail from central Thailand, the area most accessible to Westerners by way of its capital city, Bangkok. However, these universal Thai menu staples barely scratch the surface of Thai cuisine. With this book, you are given the tools you need to prepare these much-loved dishes, as well as many lesser-known Thai foods that shine with flavor and simplicity.

BELOVED THAI FOODS

Of all Thai dishes, these are some of the most well-known around the world. There are certainly many methods for preparing each, and two variations may differ as broadly as night and day, depending on where you enjoy the meal.

GREEN CURRY

Perhaps one of the most iconic dishes of Thai cuisine, green curry is in fact more beige than green. Named after the green chiles used to make the curry paste, this curry is both spicy and sweet due to the inclusion of coconut milk. Hailing from central Thailand, it is one of the region's signature dishes. Chicken and Thai eggplant are one of the most common combinations for this curry, though it can also be made using fish, fish balls, vegetables, or beef.

Like many Thai curries, green curry normally includes only one or two types of vegetable, while the actual curry is quite thin and served alongside a generous portion of jasmine rice or rice noodles. The green curry paste itself can vary considerably, depending on where it is made and who is making it, but common elements in any green curry dish include coconut cream, coconut milk, palm sugar, and fish sauce. The curry is garnished with holy basil and fresh lime leaves.

PAD THAI

A typical street food found throughout Thailand, basic pad thai consists of rice noodles stir-fried with tofu and eggs and flavored using tamarind pulp, fish sauce, chile peppers, and palm sugar. Other variations include shrimp, chicken, or pork. Pad thai is almost always served with bean sprouts, lime wedges, and cilantro.

Considered a national dish, pad thai did not gain popularity until the 1940s, when Prime Minister Plaek Phibunsongkhram worked with his government to minimize China's influence and promote nationalism: One way was to promote the new rice noodles being made in Thailand, prior to which Chinese wheat noodles were used in Thailand. Similar dishes are made in Vietnam and in the Cantonese cuisine of China; however, the unique flavors of Thai pad thai stand on their own.

SOM TAM

Papaya salad, or som tam, has many variations, but the basic musts for this sweet and spicy salad are papaya, chiles, and garlic. Traditionally made using a mortar and pestle to bruise, slightly grind, and release the juices of the ingredients, the salad can include several additions and take on many different flavors. Some of the most common cohorts include yard-long beans, dried shrimp, cherry tomatoes, preserved fish, and rice noodles. Papaya salad is mouth-wateringly spicy, and it is always served with a side of sticky rice.

Som tam originated in northeastern Thailand, in the area referred to as the Issan region. Here, foods are known for their heat, and sweet ingredients such as coconut are rarely used. However, when som tam migrated south to Bangkok, palm sugar became an often-used addition. As with most Thai foods, region dictates how this dish is prepared. Reflecting a combination seen in all areas the salad blends salty and sour to create a crisp, refreshing salad bursting with flavor.

Literally meaning "boiled salad," this is a hot and sour soup featuring a clear broth and fragrant herbs. Flavored with kaffir lime leaves, galangal, lemongrass, lime juice, crushed chile peppers, and fish sauce, this soup, like most Thai dishes, can vary widely depending on where it is served. Meats such as chicken, shrimp, pork, or beef can be used as protein, and characteristically, the soup is fiery hot.

The most popular variety of this soup today is tom yam kung, a version with shrimp that has been popularized since the influx of tourists to Thailand. More traditionally, tom yam pla, a version using white fish, was widely prepared. Tom yam is accompanied by rice, and like many Thai dishes, is most often served family style.

FLAVORFUL THAI COOKING AT ITS BEST

While Thai food is traditionally prepared using high heat in a wok or over the spit of a grill, slow cooking is just as viable an option for creating the cuisine's intense flavors. While not the traditional method for preparing Thai food, using this modern implement is a great way to consolidate steps, take out the guesswork, and produce a flavorful result that rivals your favorite restaurant.

Slow cooking allows flavors to infuse more thoroughly, endowing curries and soups with some of the same rich flavors they would normally have with a day or two of rest after cooking—but without the wait. For tougher meats like beef and pork, slow cooking can create tender results with little effort. For leaner cuts like poultry, slow cooking can lock in moisture and produce succulent curries and soups that rival those prepared traditionally.

The recipes in this book are particularly suited to your busy lifestyle. They require minimal prep work—most involve little more than measuring and chopping some ingredients and adding them to the slow cooker. To find recipes with a prep time under 15 minutes, look for the Quick Prep icon. Many recipes can also be prepped the night before to further simplify busy mornings.

Chapters 3 through 8 offer recipes specifically designed for preparation in your slow cooker. However, for obvious reasons, some dishes, such as salads, sides, and condiments, cannot be made in the slow cooker, and you will find these recipes in the final two chapters of the book, chapters 9 and 10. These are common accompaniments to the meals in this book, as well as some of the key ingredients used to make many dishes, such as curry pastes and stocks.

Of course, if you prefer not to make your own, store-bought curry pastes and soup stocks can also be used in place of the items in chapter 10. Keep in mind that variations between store-bought curry pastes and the curry paste recipes in this book can occur. For example, store-bought pastes are typically much spicier than the curry pastes outlined in this book, and therefore you will need to use a smaller quantity. When substituting store-bought curry pastes, refer to the package instructions regarding how much to use.

All recipes in this book are designed to serve four to six people, most often as part of a larger meal containing rice and at least one other side dish. Most of the side dishes in this book are simple and quick to make. They can be prepared while you wait for your main course to finish cooking, and they make easy accompaniments to the various meals outlined here.

KNOW YOUR SLOW COOKER

The recipes in this book were all developed for use in a 5- to 6-quart slow cooker. Though it's possible to substitute larger or smaller slow cookers, keep in mind that results may vary. Even among slow cookers of the suggested size, there is a wide variation among brands in terms of temperature and hot spots. Getting to know your slow cooker and how it works is particularly helpful in mastering slow cooking.

The recipes in this book vary in cooking time from 1 to 8 hours. Because the modern workday can often exceed 8 hours—and assuming you will be away from home while slow cooking—you'll do best to purchase a slow cooker that is programmable for producing the best results from these recipes. Once the cooking time is reached, a programmable slow cooker will turn to a warm setting automatically, keeping your food at a safe temperature while not overcooking the meal. If you spend long days away from the house, this is definitely the type of slow cooker you want to have.

Many recipes here provide both low and high power settings and cooking times. However, the low setting is preferable for most recipes, as it allows the flavors to develop, sauces to thicken, and meats to tenderize. Whenever possible, use the low setting for the best flavor and most consistent results.

If you are using a smaller, slower cooker and reducing the recipe size to suit your situation, decrease the cooking time by up to one-third, and begin checking for doneness on the lower end of the recommended time. However, because different slow cookers cook at different temperatures, it is important to keep an eye on your cooker, especially when trying a new recipe. Newer slow cookers tend to cook at higher temperatures than older ones, as well, so you may need to adjust the cook time further based on the age of your slow cooker.

Using Your Slow Cooker: Dos and Don'ts

DO

Prep Your Slow Cooker

Some recipes call for prepping your slow cooker with foil and cooking spray before cooking. When this is the case, don't overlook these simple steps. Otherwise, you could end up with quite a mess to clean. In some recipes, foil is also used to allow for the easy removal of certain dishes, such as meatloaf, where presentation is a factor.

DON'T

Overfill Your Slow Cooker

Most slow cookers are designed to be filled no more than two-thirds full. Be mindful of this when using your slow cooker, as filling it further can greatly affect cooking times, as well as potentially cause food safety concerns. Check with the manufacturer of your slow cooker for specific filling instructions for your model.

DO

Cook on Low

Some recipes include options for cooking foods on low or high, depending on your preference for time. To produce the moistest, most tender dishes, it's always best to use the low setting, so if time will allow, opt for low.

DON'T

Remove the Lid

It can be pretty tempting to look inside your slow cooker and see what's going on, especially once the aroma begins to fill the room. However, taking the lid off can affect overall cooking time, as it takes a considerable amount of time to heat the slow cooker back up once you've closed the lid. If you must look inside the cooker, wait until 30 to 45 minutes before the end of the cooking time to determine doneness.

DO

Follow Cooking Times

Sure, you've seen many recipes that call for cooking chicken all day or cooking beef quickly on high. However, these won't give you optimal results. Cooking chicken for longer than 6 hours can leave you with a dry, stringy result, and cooking beef on high can produce a tough-to-chew meal. If you have to be at work all day and want to make a recipe that calls for a shorter cooking time, invest in a programmable slow cooker that will switch to warm once cooking is complete. This will ensure your meal is top quality when you arrive home.

DON'T

Forget to Plan

Slow cooking saves time, but it also requires some additional planning on your part. The night before, prep the meat and any vegetables, and store them in separate containers in the refrigerator. Don't place the whole slow cooker insert in the refrigerator, as this can affect cooking time and food safety. In the morning, add the ingredients, and set the slow cooker to the necessary time.

DO

Brown Meat When Needed

It's not always necessary to brown meat before placing it in the slow cooker, and really, isn't the point of the slow cooker to cut down on prep time? Well, the truth is that sometimes it *is* necessary to brown meat for the sake of maintaining flavor after such a long cooking time. Follow the recommended directions when browning is called for, and you will be happy you did when your meat is flavorful and moist at the end of a long day.

DON'T

Pare Down on Flavor

The long cooking time in a slow cooker has a tendency to mute certain flavors. For this reason, some recipes contain greater amounts of aromatics than you may be used to using in other methods of cooking. Don't hold back, thinking that the finished product will be overwhelming. And be sure not to skimp on last minute additions such as lime juice and herbs needed to boost flavor.

DO

Use the Right Size Slow Cooker

Slow cookers come in sizes ranging from 1 to 8 quarts. While you can experiment with any size cooker, the recipes in this book work best using a 5- to 6-quart slow cooker. If you do choose to use a different size cooker, be sure to keep a closer eye on cooking times and monitor the progress to ensure that the finished product is not overdone.

DON'T

Use Frozen Meats

You may have seen recipes that tell you to put frozen meat in the slow cooker. However, don't be tempted to skip the thawing step, as this can potentially be dangerous. When foods are frozen, they take longer to cook, leaving your meat in a dangerous temperature zone for too long when cooking at such a low cooking temperature. To avoid any risk, thaw meats overnight in the refrigerator, and they will be ready for slow cooking in the morning.

2

THE THAI KITCHEN

....

When you flip to a recipe and see several unfamiliar items, it can be intimidating. And when cooking authentic Thai food, chances are you won't be able to pick up all the ingredients at your regular grocery store. A trip to an Asian market will definitely be in order, and in some cases, you may have to scour the aisles as well as the Internet to find exactly what you need.

However, don't be dismayed. As Asian foods become increasingly engrained in the fabric of America, the necessary ingredients are becoming more accessible. While you may not find everything you need at your favorite grocery store, chances are, you can locate several pieces of the puzzle there and get started on the journey of stocking your pantry Thai-style.

Stocking a Thai kitchen may seem confusing at first, but once you figure out where to source key ingredients, you will easily navigate shopping for your Thai meals. To find Thai produce, you will most likely have to shop at an Asian market. Being armed with the knowledge of exactly what you are looking for helps a great deal, so you'll find descriptions of the various produce below.

If you don't have access to an Asian market, countless mail order companies sell most of the products called for in these recipes. For help on sourcing hard-to-find ingredients, check out the Resources list (page 136). Once you stock your pantry, you will be surprised at how easy it is to cook delicious Thai food at home.

THE INGREDIENTS

Here is a closer look at the basic ingredients essential to Thai cooking. You will find these ingredients popping up in the recipes throughout this book.

BASIL: Basil is one of the most widely used herbs in Thai cooking, though European varieties are rarely used. Instead, holy basil and Thai basil are paired with everything from soups and salads to curries. Grow these varieties in your own garden, or in a pot during the warmer months, and have an ample supply, or pick them up at an Asian market, where they are readily available.

- *Holy basil:* The relation to mint is notable in holy basil, as the leaves have a similarly rough texture. Available in the spring, summer, and early fall, holy basil has small leaves with a purple tinge.

- *Thai basil:* Closely related to holy basil, Thai basil has purple stems and a stronger anise flavor than other varieties.

BEAN SPROUTS: White sprouts about 2 to 3 inches long with thin yellow tops, bean sprouts are sold in the refrigerated section of the grocery store or Asian market. Look for them in bins or bags, and be sure to inspect for quality, as they go bad quickly. Any bags containing mushy or discolored sprouts should be avoided.

BLACK SOY SAUCE: Thicker and darker than other types of soy sauce, black soy sauce has hints of molasses and a much stronger taste than thin soy sauce. You will need to purchase this at an Asian market.

CHILE-TAMARIND PASTE: This paste forms the backbone of many Thai soups and stir-fries. Many commercially produced versions are available, though the best flavor comes from making your own (page 124).

CHINESE BROCCOLI: A slender version of the broccoli you're more likely used to, Chinese broccoli is found most often at Asian grocery stores. Leafier than the more well-known varieties, Chinese broccoli is often served steamed or stir-fried. It is sometimes available seasonally in larger grocery stores and is often labeled *gai lan* in Asian markets.

CHINESE CELERY: Like Chinese broccoli, Chinese celery is also leafier and thinner than the Western varieties. Look for it at an Asian market.

CILANTRO: Cilantro gives its unique, piquant flavor to myriad Thai dishes. It can be found at many traditional grocery stores as well as any Asian market. When cooking with cilantro in Thai cuisine, both the leaves and stems are used.

COCONUT MILK AND CREAM: Coconut milk and cream are essential ingredients that add a rich creaminess to many Thai foods. Many widely distributed types of coconut milk contain emulsifiers and other additives, but for the best results, choose a brand with no added ingredients. Mae Ploy and Chaokoh are two of the best Thai brands.

FISH SAUCE: Fish sauce is one of the most vital ingredients in all of Thai cooking. Used as a substitute for salt, this fermented sauce helps combine the many flavors of Thai cooking. Fish sauce can be found in many levels of quality, with the highest grades made from shrimp or anchovies. If you are on a gluten-free diet, be sure to choose a brand labeled gluten-free, as some producers use hydrolyzed wheat proteins, labeled hydrolyzed vegetable protein, in their fish sauce.

GALANGAL: Similar in appearance to ginger, galangal is an essential ingredient in many curry pastes to which it gives its distinctive flavor. Find it in Thai or Asian markets, where it is sold both fresh and frozen.

GREEN PAPAYA: Green papaya is simply unripe papaya that has green, firm flesh. The fruit is typically only found underripe to this degree at Asian markets. In some busier markets, it is also sold freshly grated, taking some of the labor out of preparing papaya salad.

KABOCHA: A Japanese squash, kabocha has been in Thailand for centuries and makes its way into many different types of curry. Its golden flesh is solid and stands up well to slow cooking. It's become quite widely available: Along with Asian markets, kabocha can be found at many grocery stores, especially in the fall when it is harvested.

KAFFIR LIME LEAVES: Kaffir lime leaves can be found in the freezer or refrigerated section in many Asian grocery stores. Often added at the end of cooking to impart subtle lime flavor, kaffir lime leaves can be substituted with lime peel or omitted altogether. Don't bother with dried leaves, as the flavor is quite diminished. Use frozen leaves straightaway without defrosting.

LEMONGRASS: Lemongrass has become a more mainstream ingredient in recent years, making it available in some standard grocery stores, but it can always be found in an Asian market. To use lemongrass, trim the bottom half-inch from the stalk, remove a few leaves, and slice the inner, softer heart. The flavor of lemongrass quickly deteriorates in the refrigerator, so be sure to use it within a couple days of purchase for the best results.

LIME: The limes used in Thai cooking are smaller than the American lime, and their flavor more closely resembles a key lime. While regular lime juice can be substituted, key limes pack in a bit more flavor. Considering you can purchase these at most grocery stores, they really are your best option.

MANGO: With dozens of varieties available in Thailand, mangos are one of the country's most abundant fruits. Cultivated for many centuries, mangos are often paired with spicy and tart ingredients. Mangos are eaten ripe and, when unripe, used similarly to a vegetable. For the most variety, including finding unripe mangos, purchase them at an Asian grocery store.

NOODLES: The noodles used in this book can typically be found in any standard grocery store with an Asian section. In some Asian markets, you may be able to find fresh noodles, but the dried varieties are much more widely available.

- *Bean-thread vermicelli:* These white-colored, fine cellophane noodles are sold in packages consisting of several bundles of the delicate noodles. Made from mung bean starch, bean-thread noodles are tasteless and take on the flavor of whatever sauce or broth they accompany.

- *Rice noodles:* Countless shapes and sizes of rice noodles are available. The preparation of rice noodles typically involves soaking the noodles in water before use. Rice noodles can also be fried, but in this book, we will be serving them softened only.

- *Somen noodles:* A Japanese noodle variety, somen noodles are substituted for the white angel hair pasta of Thailand used in making *khanom chine*. These noodles are often served with a curry sauce and topped with fresh vegetables.

PALM SUGAR: Palm sugar brings a unique sweetness to many Thai dishes. Sold in hardened disks, it can be found at most Asian markets. Before purchasing, be sure to read the label and select a brand that contains 100 percent palm sugar. Don't substitute white sugar for this ingredient. If you can't find palm sugar, use an equal amount of light brown sugar instead.

All About Chiles

Thai food is known for its high level of spice, but it's not just any chiles that produce its unique flavor. Rather, Thai cooking carefully combines fresh and dried chiles of different varieties, so understanding which types to choose for your particular recipe is essential.

FRESH CHILES

BIRD'S EYE CHILES (THAI CHILES): These are the most commonly used type of chile in Thai cooking. At just about 2 or 3 inches long, these tiny chiles pack in a whole lot of heat. They can be found at Asian markets as well as many well-stocked grocery stores. Available in red and green varieties, each of which has its own distinct flavor, these chiles can significantly vary in heat. Before you add a generous portion to a recipe, be sure to carefully sample them to determine their heat level.

HUNGARIAN WAX AND ANAHEIM CHILES: In many Thai recipes, these larger, milder chiles are used in dishes to provide a different distinctive heat. These can both be found in major supermarkets as well as in Asian stores. Again, heat level can vary, so be sure to taste the chiles carefully before adding them to a dish.

DRIED CHILES

DRIED THAI CHILES: These are the dried variety of fresh Thai chiles, and like fresh ones, they are available in both red and green varieties and are about 2 to 3 inches in length. They are available in just about every Asian grocery store, as well as in many traditional grocery stores and online. Look for chiles that are imported from Thailand.

NEW MEXICO AND CALIFORNIA CHILES: These are two widely available larger, milder chiles that are added to many Thai curries to provide some heat, but not nearly as much as Thai chiles. New Mexico is the hotter of the two, so if you want a little more spice, but less than that of Thai chiles, choose these.

PREPARATION

Dried chiles can be prepared in many ways, but two of the most common are dry roasting and frying.

DRY ROASTING: This technique simply means that a dry pan is set over medium-high heat, and the chiles are placed in it. The heat can be decreased to medium-low once the pan is hot, and the chiles must be stirred regularly until they become uniformly darker, in about 15 minutes.

FRYING: To fry dried chiles, add a bit of vegetable oil to a pan, and stir to coat the chiles well. Turn the heat to medium, and stir the chiles continuously until they have darkened, about 10 minutes. Then remove the chiles from the oil to a paper towel to drain. The oil, which has now taken on some spice, can be used to add heat when cooking other foods.

POMELO: More fragrant than a grapefruit, the pomelo is a massive citrus fruit the size of a small melon. Growing abundantly in Thailand, this sweet fruit is available in the winter months at Asian markets.

RICE: The recipes in this book are meant to be paired with jasmine rice. Though in a pinch you certainly can use any type of rice you already have, using jasmine rice will give the meal a more authentic Thai feel. Purchase a Thai brand of rice for the best flavor.

SESAME OIL: Made from roasted sesame seeds, sesame oil has a nutty flavor that imparts a unique taste to foods. Be sure to find a brand that is 100 percent sesame oil, as many types have additional fillers.

SHALLOTS: Shallots are used in Thai cooking to add flavor to curry pastes, as well as to season the end dish while cooking. Find Asian shallots at any Asian grocery store, or substitute the French variety of shallots in equal proportion.

SHRIMP PASTE: Another integral part of Thai cooking is the flavorful and pungent shrimp paste. Made from a tiny crustacean, this dark, readily available condiment provides the salty flavor in many dishes. Look for Thai brands at an Asian market.

SPRING ROLL WRAPPERS: Paper thin, spring roll wrappers can be found in most grocery stores with an Asian food section, as well as at Asian grocery stores. A 1-pound package contains about 25 (8-inch) wrappers.

TAMARIND PASTE: Tamarind paste is generally sold in blocks of dried pulp. To use it, you will need to make an extract by soaking the pulp in hot water.

THAI EGGPLANTS: While any small Asian eggplant can be substituted for Thai eggplants, going the extra step to get Thai eggplants is definitely worth the effort. Look for these at any Asian grocery store. About the size of a ping-pong ball, they can range in color from white to green to yellow.

THIN SOY SAUCE: Lighter than standard soy sauce, thin soy sauce is an often-used Thai ingredient that adds a subtle tone to many dishes. This sauce is not thick or sweet, and it has a dark caramel color. Avoid substituting a low-sodium soy sauce here, as this is not the same thing. Look for a Thai variety of thin soy sauce, such as Healthy Boy or Maekrua.

TURMERIC ROOT: A yellow root with a similar appearance to ginger, turmeric root has a strikingly bright inner flesh. Find it at Asian or Indian markets, as well as some high-end specialty grocery stores.

WHITE PEPPERCORNS: White peppercorns, which are slightly hotter than black peppercorns, are used in place of black peppercorns in Thai cooking. Find white peppercorns at a well-stocked grocery store or Asian market. For the most flavor, when a recipe calls for freshly ground white pepper, grind it fresh from peppercorns in a spice grinder or mortar.

YARD-LONG BEANS: You won't need a sign to spot yard-long beans. They are—simply put—just really long green beans. Ranging from 2 to 3 feet, these beans are great in a stir-fry or curry. Look for beans with a bright green color without darkened spots. Find them at Asian grocery stores.

YELLOW BEAN SAUCE: Made by salting and fermenting crushed soybeans, yellow bean sauce can be found at any Asian grocery store. Sometimes labeled as brown bean sauce or white bean sauce, it is typically packaged in tall, long-neck bottles.

ESSENTIAL KITCHEN TOOLS

Overall, Thai cuisine is built on simplicity. You don't need a bunch of fancy implements to get cooking, especially when you already have your slow cooker handy.

- *Mortar and Pestle:* A mortar and pestle are nice tools to have. While taking a bit more time than a modern food processor, they give you a taste of the authentic preparation of many Thai foods. Used to grind

All About Fish Sauce

While the name implies otherwise, fish sauce is actually not all that fishy. Made through the fermentation of fish, its strongest attribute is saltiness. Called *nam pla* in Thai, fish sauce is used to flavor countless dishes in Southeastern Asian cuisine. It can be used as a marinade for meat and fish, and as a condiment for just about anything. Fish sauce is basically omnipresent in all Thai dishes, lending its distinctive flavor in the same way Westerners use salt and pepper at the table.

Fermented for just over one year, fish sauce can be prepared using anchovies, a variety of fish, or squid. Fish sauce should only contain three ingredients: fish, water, and salt. Anything else is unnecessary and should be avoided. You'll find many brands and types of available fish sauce, and like many other

food products, not all are created equal. Look for fish sauce made in Thailand or Vietnam to use when making the dishes in this book. Be sure to check the label's ingredients to ensure you are getting a quality fish sauce without added fillers and unnecessary ingredients.

Fish sauce can be found in the Asian food section of many major grocery stores across the country. However, in several cases, the brands carried in major supermarkets are not actually made in Thailand and therefore lack some of the desired flavor and complexity. At an Asian grocery store, on the other hand, you have countless options when selecting fish sauce, so whenever possible, that is where you should go. Prices are considerably less expensive per ounce, and you will find an authentic-tasting fish sauce for use in your cooking.

For vegetarians, simply substitute an equal quantity of Golden Mountain Sauce or thin soy sauce in exchange for fish sauce. While the taste will differ slightly, these are the closest replacements for fish sauce when cooking Thai food. If an Asian grocery store is not accessible to you, these items can be ordered online.

spices for curry pastes, the mortar is a marble bowl, and the pestle is a rounded tool used to smash foods placed in the mortar.

- *Food Processor:* If you don't have a mortar and pestle, a food processor provides an easy stand-in and gets the job done in record speed. If you plan on making any of the curry pastes in this book, you will need either a food processor or mortar and pestle. If time is a factor, a food processor is the most logical option. When fitted with a shredding blade, a food processor can also be used to shred papaya for making papaya salad in record time.

BASIC KITCHEN TOOLS

Beyond the above items, you'll need some basic kitchen items to prepare the recipes, many of which are most likely in your kitchen already.

- *Ladle:* for serving many of the items from the slow cooker.

- *Kitchen shears:* particularly useful for a variety of kitchen prep work tasks, especially when handling meat, poultry, and fish.

- *Good set of knives*

- *Pans of various sizes*

- *Wok or sauté pan:* for browning meats on the stove top to lock in flavor.

- *Large spoon and spatula*

- *Mixing bowls:* to prepare marinades and salads.

- *Aluminum foil:* used sparingly in some cooking processes. When it is called for, be sure to use it, as it makes a great difference in quality and results.

SPECIALIZED KITCHEN TOOLS

Though not absolute requirements, you'll find the following specialized items helpful in cooking Thai dishes as well.

- *Soup tureen:* a great serving dish for Thai soups. Traditionally, soups are served family style at the table and ladled into individual bowls as part of a larger meal.

- *Vegetable peeler:* designed to shred vegetables, this is helpful for preparing papaya salad, especially if you don't have a food processor. Look for it in the utensil section of an Asian grocery store, where it's readily available.

- *Rice cooker:* an invaluable component to streamlined meal preparation. It is certainly possible to cook rice in any saucepan with a tight-fitting lid, but having a rice cooker makes perfect rice possible every time. And with varieties that can be programmed to have rice ready when you need it, this is a simple, relatively inexpensive investment in your kitchen. Even with heavy use, most rice cookers will last many years and are well worth the cost.

PART TWO

Recipes

3

SOUPS

....

Curried Kabocha Coconut Soup

kaeng liang fak thong

SOY-FREE | NUT-FREE **This rich soup is a royal treat, providing much of the same appeal as shrimp bisque—with a Thai twist. In this traditional Thai dish, the kabocha is left in small, bite-size pieces. If you prefer, skip the immersion blender step for a more textured soup. Before serving, finish the soup by adding coconut milk to produce its characteristic creaminess.**

SERVES 4 TO 6
PREP TIME: 15 MINUTES
COOK TIME: 6 HOURS ON LOW,
3 HOURS ON HIGH

¾ cup dried shrimp

2 pounds kabocha

¼ cup Red Curry Paste (page 128) or store bought

4 cups Chicken Stock (page 118) or store bought, divided

1 (13.5-ounce) can unsweetened coconut milk

½ cup loosely packed fresh Thai basil

2 Thai or serrano chiles (optional)

1 lime, for garnish

Serving tip: Many Thai dishes like soups and curries use both fresh and dried chiles in their preparation. The nuanced heat of fresh chiles provides a unique flavor when added at the end of cooking. For less heat while still retaining this authentic Thai flavor, use milder chiles at the end of cooking as a garnish.

1. Soak the dried shrimp in cold water for 10 minutes while you prepare the other ingredients.

2. Cut the kabocha in half, and remove the seeds. Using a sharp knife, remove as much skin as possible, cut the kabocha into chunks, and place them in the slow cooker.

3. In a food processor, grind the shrimp and Red Curry Paste together. Add a little Chicken Stock to the bowl to help create an evenly ground paste. Once complete, mix 1 cup of Chicken Stock into the paste and stir well to incorporate. Add this mixture to the slow cooker along with the remaining 3 cups of Chicken Stock.

4. Cook on low for 6 hours or high for 3 hours.

5. Before serving, remove the lid, and use an immersion blender to purée the soup. Pour in the can of coconut milk, and add the basil to the slow cooker. Add the Thai or serrano chiles (if using). Continue to cook the soup on low with the lid off for about 5 minutes, or until heated through.

6. Ladle the soup into a tureen or individual bowls, garnish with the lime, and serve.

Hot and Sour Shrimp Soup

tom yum kung

SOY-FREE | NUT-FREE | QUICK PREP Tom Yum is made so many different ways that no two batches are really ever alike. Simultaneously spicy, tart, and sweet, this soup grows on you the more you eat it. Try it along with rice to cut some of the heat, or eat it throughout a meal for a welcome contrast.

SERVES 4 TO 6
PREP TIME: 10 MINUTES
COOK TIME: 6 HOURS ON LOW,
2 HOURS ON HIGH

6 cups Chicken Stock (page 118)
  or store bought
1 stalk lemongrass, trimmed and cut
  into thin slices
Rind of 1 key lime
2 tablespoons homemade Chile-
  Tamarind Paste (page 125)
  or store bought
1 cup quartered button mushrooms
3 to 5 Thai chiles, thinly sliced
1 pound medium shrimp
¼ cup fish sauce
½ cup freshly squeezed lime juice
¼ cup palm sugar
Cilantro, for garnish

1. In the slow cooker, stir together the Chicken Stock, lemongrass, lime rind, Chile-Tamarind Paste, mushrooms, and Thai chiles.

2. Cook on low for 6 hours, or on high for 2 hours.

3. Adjust the heat to high, and add the shrimp, fish sauce, lime juice, and palm sugar, and cook for 10 minutes more, or until the shrimp are uniformly pink.

4. Ladle the soup into a tureen or individual bowls, garnish with the cilantro, and serve.

Serving tip: A common seasoning used in Thai cuisine, lemongrass is meant to add flavor. It shouldn't be eaten by itself. If you are having guests, be sure to inform them of this, as the pieces can be quite rough on the throat if swallowed.

Tamarind Shrimp Curry Soup

kaeng som kung sod

SOY-FREE | NUT-FREE   With a saucy texture somewhere between a soup and a curry, this simple soup uses a special sour curry paste as its base. The paste itself is not overtly sour, but when paired with tamarind, as it most often is, it takes on an intensely sour yet delightful flavor. Prepare the simple paste the night before, so the soup can begin its slow cook before you head out the door in the morning.

SERVES 4 TO 6
PREP TIME: 15 MINUTES
COOK TIME: 6 HOURS ON LOW,
2 HOURS ON HIGH

FOR THE CURRY PASTE

4 dried red New Mexico chiles
1 teaspoon shrimp paste
2 medium shrimp,
    peeled and deveined
2 tablespoons chopped garlic
¼ cup chopped shallots

FOR THE SOUP

4 cups Chicken Stock (page 118)
    or store bought, plus 1 cup for
    grinding (if needed)
3 tablespoons fish sauce
2 tablespoons palm sugar
6 tablespoons Tamarind Water
    (page 124)
1 head napa cabbage
½ pound medium shrimp,
    peeled and deveined

TO MAKE THE CURRY PASTE

In a food processor, grind the chiles, shrimp paste, shrimp, garlic, and shallots until they are a fine paste. If using a food processor, add 1 cup of Chicken Stock to aid in the grinding.

TO MAKE THE SOUP

1. In the slow cooker, stir together the curry paste, the Chicken Stock, fish sauce, palm sugar, and Tamarind Water.

2. Cook on low for 6 hours, or on high for 2 hours.

3. Remove and discard the outer leaves of the napa cabbage. Dice the remaining inner, more tender leaves.

4. Adjust the heat to high. Add the shrimp and napa cabbage to the slow cooker, replace the lid, and continue cooking the soup for 10 minutes.

5. Ladle the soup into a tureen or individual bowls and serve.

Storage tip: Leftover soups can be stored in the refrigerator in an airtight container. Place any leftovers in a storage container to cool, and then refrigerate once they are room temperature. To enjoy the most robust flavor from leftover soups, plan on eating the leftovers within 2 days of preparation. To reheat, bring to a gentle simmer on the stove before serving.

Orange Fish Soup ～ *gem som pla*

SOY-FREE | NUT-FREE Seamlessly melding sweet, spicy, and sour attributes, this classic Thai soup highlights just one of the many ways in which white fish is prepared in Thai cooking. Make the paste the night before for easy prep in the morning, and pour a glass of wine as the fish finishes cooking right before serving, completely fuss-free.

SERVES 4 TO 6
PREP TIME: 15 MINUTES
COOK TIME: 6 HOURS ON LOW,
2 HOURS ON HIGH

FOR THE PASTE

½ teaspoon shrimp paste
4 garlic cloves
2 red Thai chiles
1 tablespoon fish sauce
2 shallots, peeled
2-inch piece galangal
¼ teaspoon white peppercorns

FOR THE SOUP

6 cups Chicken Stock (page 118)
   or store bought
1 tablespoon palm sugar
1 tablespoon Tamarind Water
   (page 124)
1 small zucchini, peeled and cut into
   matchsticks
2 cups coarsely chopped bok choy
¼ cup green beans, cut into
   1-inch pieces
3 tablespoons fish sauce
3 sole fillets
1 small orange

TO MAKE THE PASTE

In a blender, food processor, or mortar, process the shrimp paste, garlic, chiles, fish sauce, shallots, galangal, and white peppercorns until a moist, smooth paste forms.

TO MAKE THE SOUP

1. Transfer the paste to the slow cooker, and stir in the Chicken Stock.

2. Add the palm sugar and Tamarind Water, and cook on low for 6 hours, or on high for 2 hours.

3. Adjust the heat to high (if you were using the low setting), and add the zucchini, bok choy, green beans, fish sauce, and sole fillets. Peel the orange, and squeeze the juice from 2 segments into the soup. Stir to combine, replace the cover, and allow to cook for about 10 additional minutes, until the fish flakes.

4. Cut the remaining orange segments in half. Serve the soup in bowls topped with 1 or 2 orange segments.

Chicken Coconut Soup *tom kha kai*

SOY-FREE | NUT-FREE | QUICK PREP This creamy, popular soup is a sure winner with crowds. Sweet and spicy, it makes a great introduction to Thai food and is universally appealing. The two most common varieties of tom kha are chicken and shrimp. If you prefer seafood to poultry, substitute shrimp for the chicken, or use a combination of the two for a rich, filling treat.

SERVES 4 TO 6
PREP TIME: 10 MINUTES
COOK TIME: 4 TO 6 HOURS ON LOW

5 cups Chicken Stock (page 118) or store bought
2 tablespoons Chile-Tamarind Paste (page 125) or store bought
¼ cup sliced galangal
1 stalk lemongrass, bottom inch removed and discarded, remaining softer portion thinly sliced
Rind of 1 key lime
¼ cup freshly squeezed lemon juice
2 tablespoons palm sugar
1 cup quartered button mushrooms
1 pound boneless, skinless chicken breasts
3 tablespoons fish sauce
2 (13.5-ounce) cans unsweetened coconut milk
5 Thai chiles
Cilantro, for garnish

1. In the slow cooker, stir together the Chicken Stock, Chile-Tamarind Paste, galangal, lemongrass, key lime rind, lemon juice, palm sugar, and button mushrooms. Nestle the chicken breasts on top of the mixture.

2. Cook on low for 4 to 6 hours.

3. Using two forks, gently shred the chicken.

4. Add the fish sauce and coconut milk to the slow cooker, stirring to combine. Cover and cook on low for 10 more minutes, until the coconut milk is heated through. Using the side of a knife, crush the chiles lightly, and add them to the soup.

5. Ladle the soup into a large tureen or individual bowls and serve garnished with cilantro.

Ingredient tip: Coconut milk is a great source of lauric acid and capric acid and is high in iron, phosphorus, and zinc. Considered a warming food in Chinese medicine, coconut supports the heart, spleen, large intestine, and stomach and is used in natural medicine to soothe internal membranes. Because the coconut is naturally sweet, it is best to avoid using any type of sweetened coconut milk and choose varieties that do not have unnecessary additives.

Ground Pork and Spinach Soup

kaeng chued pak bung chin mu sub

SOY-FREE | NUT-FREE | QUICK PREP Flavored with white pepper and fish sauce, this simple soup is distinctive for its salty, subtle taste. Make the meatballs the night before, and then place everything in the slow cooker in the morning. Because the meatballs have nothing to hold them together, they will crumble slightly during cooking. This is to be expected, and it adds to the charm of the home-style soup. Right before serving, finish the soup by adding the spinach, giving it just enough time to wilt while still retaining its bright green hue.

SERVES 4 TO 6
PREP TIME: 10 MINUTES
COOK TIME: 4 TO 6 HOURS ON LOW

½ pound ground pork

¼ cup chopped garlic

½ teaspoon freshly ground
   white pepper

½ tablespoon sugar

2 tablespoons fish sauce

6 cups Chicken Stock (page 118)
   or store bought

1 pound spinach

1. In a small bowl, mix the pork, garlic, white pepper, sugar, and fish sauce together using clean hands. To tenderize the meat, bang it several times against the side of the bowl as you mix the ingredients together. Break the pork mixture off into small, uneven-size meatballs. Place the meatballs in the slow cooker, and add the Chicken Stock.

2. Cook on low for 4 to 6 hours.

3. About 5 minutes before serving, add the spinach, replace the lid, and let the soup cook until the spinach has wilted.

4. Ladle the soup into a tureen or individual bowls and serve.

Pork Rib and Greens Soup — *phak kad jaw*

SOY-FREE | NUT-FREE   This Northern Thai comfort soup is teeming with rich, soured flavor. The long, slow cook tenderizes the pork and adds massive seasoning to the broth. Unlike many other soups, this one starts with just water instead of a premade stock. To add more heat, top the soup with a few dried fried chiles before serving.

SERVES 4 TO 6
PREP TIME: 15 MINUTES
COOK TIME: 6 TO 8 HOURS ON LOW

FOR THE PASTE

4 dried Thai chiles

1 teaspoon salt

10 garlic cloves

5 shallots

1 tablespoon shrimp paste

1 cup water

FOR THE SOUP

5 cups water

1½ pounds pork spareribs, cut into
    individual ribs

1 small onion, cut into thin wedges

1 teaspoon salt

1 pound mustard greens, washed and
    cut into 2-inch pieces

½ cup Tamarind Water (page 124)

1 tablespoon fish sauce

1½ teaspoons yellow bean sauce

2 tablespoons Crispy Shallots
    (page 126)

TO MAKE THE PASTE

In the jar of a food processor, process the chiles, salt, garlic, shallots, and shrimp paste until smooth, adding the water to the jar to aid in mixing. Transfer to a slow cooker.

TO MAKE THE SOUP

1. Add the water to the slow cooker, and stir to combine with the paste. Add the pork spareribs, onion, salt, and mustard greens.

2. Cook on low for 6 to 8 hours.

3. About 20 minutes before serving, add the Tamarind Water, fish sauce, and yellow bean sauce, and replace the cover. Cook for an additional 10 minutes, until heated through. Adjust the seasonings if necessary by adding more fish sauce, yellow bean sauce, and Tamarind Water.

4. Ladle into individual bowls, and serve topped with the Crispy Shallots.

Ingredient tip: Mustard greens can range in spiciness from mildly piquant to overwhelmingly hot. Thankfully, most commercial varieties are on the milder end of the spectrum. Curled mustard greens are the type most readily available from grocery stores, and they are notable for their jade green, crinkled leaves. In an Asian grocery store, look for the greens labeled *yu choy*.

Coconut Cauliflower-Leek Soup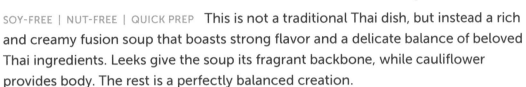

SOY-FREE | NUT-FREE | QUICK PREP This is not a traditional Thai dish, but instead a rich and creamy fusion soup that boasts strong flavor and a delicate balance of beloved Thai ingredients. Leeks give the soup its fragrant backbone, while cauliflower provides body. The rest is a perfectly balanced creation.

SERVES 4 TO 6
PREP TIME: 10 MINUTES
COOK TIME: 4 TO 6 HOURS ON LOW

4 cups chopped leeks, washed several times

6 cups Chicken Stock (page 118)

6 cups chopped cauliflower florets

2 carrots, grated

1 stalk lemongrass, bottom inch removed and discarded, remaining softer portion thinly sliced

1-inch ginger knob, grated

1 (13.5-ounce) can unsweetened coconut milk

¼ cup fish sauce

¼ cup loosely packed Thai basil

1. In the slow cooker, stir together the leeks, chicken stock, cauliflower florets, carrots, lemongrass, and ginger.

2. Cook on low for 4 to 6 hours.

3. Add the coconut milk and fish sauce, stir and cover. Cook for 10 more minutes.

4. Add the Thai basil and stir until it is just wilted.

5. Ladle the soup into a large tureen or individual bowls.

4

NOODLES AND RICE

....

Jasmine Rice

SOY-FREE | NUT-FREE | QUICK PREP While main courses always seem to fill the slow cooker, don't overlook the versatile tool's value to create perfectly cooked rice with ease. Unlike with some other dishes, where you can set it and forget it, cooking rice in a slow cooker requires a bit more attention, especially toward the end of cooking. However, once you have the timing down for your particular slow cooker, feel free to use the programming feature, and keep it warm until serving time.

SERVES 6
PREP TIME: 5 MINUTES
COOK TIME: 2 TO 3 HOURS ON HIGH

Nonstick cooking spray
3 cups jasmine rice
4½ cups water or stock

Ingredient tip: Jasmine rice is a floral, long-grained rice with a tender texture. Traditionally grown in Thailand, several varieties of jasmine rice are now grown in the United States. While you can substitute other long-grained white rice varieties, they will not have the same distinct aroma as jasmine rice. If you are unable to source it at your local grocery store, visit an Asian grocer or purchase it online.

1. Spray the sides of the slow cooker with nonstick cooking spray.

2. In a small bowl, cover the rice in cold water. Rub the rice between your fingers until the water becomes cloudy, and pour the water out. Repeat this process two or three more times, until the water remains clear.

3. Add the rice and the water to the slow cooker, and cook on high for 2 to 3 hours. In the last hour of cooking time, check the rice to determine doneness.

4. Fluff the rice with a fork and serve.

Coconut Rice

SOY-FREE | NUT-FREE | QUICK PREP Coconut rice is a rich treat that pairs especially well with fiery hot curries. The cooling sweetness of coconut enhances any meal, adding a bit of flair to your dining experience. For even more flavor, add extra unsweetened coconut before cooking.

SERVES 4 TO 6
PREP TIME: 5 MINUTES
COOK TIME: 2 TO 3 HOURS ON HIGH

Nonstick cooking spray

3 cups jasmine rice

3 cups coconut milk

1¾ cups water

½ teaspoon salt

4 tablespoons shredded
    unsweetened coconut

Ingredient tip: Be sure not to exchange sweetened shredded coconut for the unsweetened coconut called for here, as it will create a cloyingly sweet result. Instead, look for dried, unsweetened coconut in the baking section of a well-stocked grocery store, or check the freezer section of an Asian market.

1. Spray the slow cooker with nonstick cooking spray.

2. In a small bowl, cover the rice in cold water. Rub the rice between your fingers until the water becomes cloudy, and pour the water out. Repeat this process two or three more times, until the water remains clear.

3. In the slow cooker, mix together the rice, coconut milk, water, salt, and coconut.

4. Cover and cook on high for 2 to 3 hours, until the rice is tender. In the last hour of cooking time, check the rice to determine doneness.

5. Before serving, fluff the rice with a fork.

Basic Congee ~ *chok*

NUT-FREE | QUICK PREP Every country where rice is a staple of the cuisine has a recipe for some variety of congee. An excellent home remedy for someone feeling under the weather, congee is the Asian equivalent to American chicken noodle soup. Easy to digest, nutritious, and delicious, congee goes by many names, including rice porridge, *jook*, and *chok*, as it is called in Thailand. Congee can be eaten for breakfast, or even a simple dinner when topped with some added protein.

SERVES 4 TO 6
PREP TIME: 5 MINUTES
COOK TIME: 8 HOURS ON LOW,
4 HOURS ON HIGH

Nonstick cooking spray

1 cup jasmine rice

½ teaspoon salt

8 cups Chicken Stock (page 118)
   or Pork Stock (page 120),
   or store bought

SUGGESTED TOPPINGS

Poached or raw eggs

Pickled vegetables

Steamed greens

Fish sauce

Soy sauce

Chili paste

1. Spray the slow cooker with nonstick cooking spray.

2. In a small bowl, cover the rice with water. Rub the rice between your fingers until the water becomes cloudy. Pour the water out, and repeat this process two or three more times, until the water remains clear. Transfer the rice to the slow cooker.

3. In the slow cooker, mix together the rice, salt, and Chicken Stock.

4. Cook on low for 8 hours, or on high for 4 hours.

5. Serve in bowls garnished with desired toppings.

Ingredient tip: Many brands of rice suggest that you don't rinse the rice before cooking, but washing rice can actually remove starch, tapioca, glucose, and other coatings commonly used in processing to give the rice sheen. While some organic rice producers avoid the use of additives, others do include them. Check labels closely if you wish to avoid this step, and when in doubt, contact the producer directly to determine their practices.

Ginger Pork Congee

chok mu

SOY-FREE | NUT-FREE | QUICK PREP This congee makes a simple but tasty meal at the beginning or end of the day. While American cuisine often includes sweet items for breakfast, in Thai cooking, breakfast is more often than not an occasion for savory fare. Let this slow cook overnight to eat on a busy morning, or come home and enjoy this comforting cross between a stew and soup after a long day.

SERVES 4 TO 6
PREP TIME: 10 MINUTES
COOK TIME: 8 HOURS ON LOW, 4 HOURS ON HIGH

Nonstick cooking spray

1 cup jasmine rice

8 cups Chicken Stock (page 118) or Pork Stock (page 120), or store bought

5 dried shiitake mushrooms, reconstituted

3 (2-inch-by-1-inch) ginger knobs, sliced ⅛-inch thick

1 cup shredded, cooked pork

½ cup thinly sliced scallions

Fish sauce, for seasoning

Freshly ground white pepper

1. Spray the slow cooker with nonstick cooking spray.

2. In a small bowl, cover the rice in cold water. Rub the rice between your fingers until the water becomes cloudy, and pour the water out. Repeat this process two or three more times, until the water remains clear.

3. In the slow cooker, stir together the rice, Chicken Stock, mushrooms, and ginger. Cook on low for 8 hours, or on high for 4 hours.

4. About 30 minutes before serving, stir in the pork.

5. Ladle the congee into individual bowls. Top with scallions, season with fish sauce and white pepper, and serve.

Ingredient tip: Shiitake mushrooms help rid the body of phlegm and mucus while supporting the liver, spleen, and stomach, making them an important medicinal ingredient to keep in your kitchen. Rich in vitamins D, B_2, and B_{12}, they also contain antiviral and antitumor qualities, qualifying them as a perfect addition to this healing congee. Find them fresh and dried at most grocery stores, health food stores, and specialty stores. When dried, soak them in warm water for 2 hours or as long as overnight before using.

Rice Soup ～ *khao tom*

NUT-FREE | QUICK PREP Another classic comfort food, rice soup differs from congee in that it starts out with a thin broth, to which the cooked rice is added at the end. A savory combination of fish sauce, pork, egg, and ginger makes this an equally filling meal for breakfast, lunch, or dinner. Use leftover rice from last night's dinner (preferred), or prepare rice in your rice cooker shortly before serving.

SERVES 4
PREP TIME: 10 MINUTES
COOK TIME: 6 TO 8 HOURS ON LOW,
5 TO 7 HOURS ON HIGH

8 cups Pork Stock (page 120)
  or store bought
1-inch ginger knob, cut into
  matchsticks
2 shallots, thinly sliced
1 stalk lemongrass, outer leaves and
  bottom inch removed and discarded,
  cut into 2-inch sections
½ pound ground pork
4 eggs
4 cups cooked jasmine rice
4 tablespoons fish sauce
4 tablespoons thin soy sauce
1 stalk Chinese celery, chopped
2 scallions, chopped
¼ cup chopped cilantro leaves

1. In the slow cooker, stir together the Pork Stock, ginger, shallots, lemongrass, and ground pork.

2. Cook on low for 6 to 8 hours, or on high for 5 to 7 hours.

3. Bring a kettle of water to a boil. In a medium bowl, arrange the uncracked eggs and pour the water over them. Leave the eggs for 10 to 15 minutes, depending on your preference for egg doneness.

4. Add the rice, fish sauce, and soy sauce to the slow cooker, and continue to cook for 10 minutes. Ladle the soup into serving bowls. Immediately crack the eggs into the bowls.

5. Top with the Chinese celery, scallions, and cilantro, and serve.

Serving tip: While Thai restaurants often have chopsticks available in the United States, in Thailand, chopstick use is limited to noodle dishes. Serve this and other dishes without noodles like the Thais do: with a spoon. All curries (with the exception of those including noodles) and soups in this book should be served with a spoon, and when needed, a fork. Because the spoon is more functional in scooping up the many saucy and soupy dishes of Thai cuisine, it is the most commonly used type of cutlery.

Thai Chicken Noodle Soup

SOY-FREE | NUT-FREE | QUICK PREP This Thai version of chicken noodle soup provides the same comfort as the classic variety, but with a distinctly Thai twist. Use leftover chicken from a previous meal, or if none is available, add a chicken breast when you place the stock in the slow cooker, and shred it with two forks before serving.

SERVES 4 TO 6
PREP TIME: 10 MINUTES
COOK TIME: 4 TO 6 HOURS ON LOW

5 cups Chicken Stock (page 118) or store bought

2-inch ginger knob, cut into matchsticks

1 Thai chile, stemmed and gently crushed

1 tablespoon Tamarind Water (page 124)

1 teaspoon turmeric

1 package thin rice noodles

2 tablespoons freshly squeezed lime juice

2 tablespoons fish sauce

1 teaspoon palm sugar

2 cans coconut milk

1 cup shredded, cooked chicken

¼ cup chopped cilantro

1. In the slow cooker, stir together the Chicken Stock, ginger, chile, Tamarind Water, and turmeric.

2. Cook on low for 4 to 6 hours.

3. Bring a large pot of water to a boil, and cook the noodles briefly until just tender, about 2 to 3 minutes.

4. Stir in the lime juice, fish sauce, palm sugar, coconut milk, and cooked chicken, and allow the ingredients to heat through for about 10 minutes.

5. Divide the rice noodles among serving bowls, and ladle the soup over them. Garnish with the cilantro and serve.

Ingredient tip: While thin rice noodles are ideal in this soup, any type of noodle can work well here. If using thicker noodles, keep in mind they may need more time to cook. To ensure they are tender, boil them for the appropriate time according to package directions before adding to the bowls.

Beef Noodle Soup ⟋ *gwaytio nuea nam*

NUT-FREE | QUICK PREP As a comfort classic, beef noodle soup is a standout. Using a beef shank allows you to set your slow cooker for up to 8 hours, making this a perfect, nourishing indulgence for the end of a long day away from home. To accompany this simple soup, prepare plenty of scallions, bean sprouts, cilantro, and Crispy Garlic (page 127) for added character and appeal.

SERVES 6
PREP TIME: 10 MINUTES
COOK TIME: 6 TO 8 HOURS ON LOW,
5 TO 7 HOURS ON HIGH

8 cups water

3 celery stalks

4 garlic cloves, peeled and
   lightly crushed

5 slices galangal

1 stalk lemongrass, outer leaves and
   bottom inch removed and discarded,
   cut into 2-inch pieces

1 cinnamon stick

3 star anise pods

1 tablespoon white peppercorns

1 bunch fresh cilantro stems,
   leaves reserved for garnish

¼ cup thin soy sauce

1½ teaspoons salt

1½ tablespoons light brown sugar

2 pounds beef shank

1 package thin rice noodles

Cilantro leaves, for garnish

Crispy Garlic (page 127), for garnish

Sliced scallions, for garnish

Bean sprouts, for garnish

1. In the slow cooker, stir together the water, celery, garlic, galangal, lemongrass, cinnamon, star anise, white peppercorns, cilantro stems, soy sauce, salt, light brown sugar, and beef shank.

2. Cook on low for 6 to 8 hours, or on high for 5 to 7 hours.

3. Strain the soup into a large bowl, reserving the meat. When cool enough to handle, remove the meat from the bone, and add it to the broth.

4. Bring a large pot of water to a boil, and cook the noodles briefly until tender, about 3 to 5 minutes.

5. Divide the rice noodles and beef among serving bowls, and spoon the broth over the top. Garnish with cilantro, Crispy Garlic, scallions, and bean sprouts and serve.

Cooking tip: Bean sprouts, most typically from the mung bean, are a commonly used garnish for a variety of Thai dishes. They do not keep very well, however, and can quickly become mushy, so only purchase the amount you intend to use within a couple of days. Before serving, always rinse the bean sprouts in fresh, cool water, and remove any of the bean seeds that float to the top.

Tofu Glass Noodle Soup

kaeng joot woon sen

NUT-FREE | QUICK PREP Playing on the contrast of tofu and pork, this soup can serve either as a tasty accompaniment or a stand-alone meal. As with all Thai meatballs, uniformity is not the key. Instead, pork balls that vary in size give the soup character. Because no filler holds them together, the balls will lose some of their shape during cooking.

SERVES 4 TO 6
PREP TIME: 10 MINUTES
COOK TIME: 6 TO 8 HOURS ON LOW,
4 TO 6 HOURS ON HIGH

6 cups Pork Stock (page 120)
   or store bought
4 garlic cloves, smashed
5 small dried mushrooms, soaked in
   water for 10 minutes and chopped
1 teaspoon freshly ground
   white pepper
½ pound ground pork
6 ounces dried glass noodles
2 tablespoons fish sauce
2 tablespoons thin soy sauce
1 teaspoon palm sugar
1 package soft tofu, chopped into
   1-inch pieces
5 scallions, chopped
¼ cup chopped fresh cilantro

1. In a slow cooker, stir together the Pork Stock, garlic, and dried mushrooms.

2. In a small bowl, mix together the white pepper and pork. Pinch off small balls into the broth in the slow cooker.

3. Cook on low for 6 to 8 hours, or on high for 4 to 6 hours.

4. In a large bowl, soak the glass noodles for 10 minutes in cold water.

5. Add the fish sauce, soy sauce, palm sugar, and tofu 10 minutes before serving.

6. Drain the noodles, and add them to the slow cooker to quickly heat through.

7. Serve in individual bowls topped with scallions and cilantro.

Cooking tip: Because the tofu in this recipe is added at the end of cooking, soft tofu is a great choice for its smooth texture. If you prefer firm or extra-firm tofu, however, you can certainly substitute it for an equally successful dish.

Curry Noodle Soup ~ *khao soi*

SOY-FREE | NUT-FREE | QUICK PREP On a cold day, a big bowl of curry noodle soup is just the thing to keep you warm. Make the paste the night before, so in the morning you can simply throw it in the slow cooker along with the stock. If you'd like a bit more substance, add a couple chicken thighs or breasts at the start of cooking, and shred them with two forks before serving.

SERVES 4 TO 6
PREP TIME: 10 MINUTES
COOK TIME: 6 TO 8 HOURS ON LOW,
2 TO 4 HOURS ON HIGH

¼ cup chopped fresh ginger

6 garlic cloves

¼ cup Red Curry Paste (page 128)
 or store bought

4 cups Chicken Stock (page 118)
 or Vegetable Stock (page 119),
 or store bought, divided

12 ounces thin rice noodles

2 (13.5-ounce) cans coconut milk

¼ cup chopped fresh Thai basil

¼ cup chopped fresh cilantro

1. In a food processor, process the ginger, garlic, and Red Curry Paste until smooth, adding 1 cup of Chicken Stock to the jar to aid in grinding. Transfer to the slow cooker. Add the remaining 3 cups of stock, and stir to combine.

2. Cook for 6 to 8 hours on low, or 2 to 4 hours on high.

3. Add the noodles and coconut milk to the slow cooker 30 minutes before serving.

4. Divide the noodles among serving bowls, and ladle the soup over them. Garnish with the Thai basil and cilantro, and serve.

Cooking tip: For Thai recipes made in a slow cooker, coconut milk is added at the end to prevent curdling. When Thai curries are quick-cooked on the stove, curdling is not an issue, but slow-cooking coconut milk can create an unappetizing appearance, as it curdles in the same way as cow's milk. For this reason, always add the coconut milk at the end of the cooking process, and continue to cook until heated through.

Pad Thai

pad thai

SOY-FREE | QUICK PREP This is by no means a traditional Thai recipe, but a remake of a classic, designed to withstand the lengthy cooking time of a slow cooker. Try this simple preparation to have a tempting chicken pad thai on the table with surprisingly little work. Peanuts are typically a condiment served with pad thai, but here they lend their flavor to the meat, whose outstanding taste still holds up after the many hours of cooking.

SERVES 6

PREP TIME: 10 MINUTES

COOK TIME: 7 HOURS ON LOW

2 chicken breasts

½ cup chunky peanut butter

½ cup fish sauce

¼ cup freshly squeezed lime juice

2 tablespoons palm sugar

2 tablespoons Sriracha

2 cups water

1 package pad thai noodles

½ pound medium shrimp,
   peeled and deveined

¼ cup bean sprouts

¼ cup sliced scallions

Crushed peanuts, for garnish

1. In the slow cooker, stir together the chicken breasts, peanut butter, fish sauce, lime juice, palm sugar, Sriracha, and water.

2. Cook on low for 6 hours, and then shred the chicken breasts with two forks.

3. Adjust the temperature to high, add the noodles, and continue to cook for an additional hour.

4. About 10 minutes before serving, add the shrimp, and cook until they are opaque. Add the bean sprouts and stir to combine.

5. Ladle into serving bowls. Serve topped with scallions and crushed peanuts.

Chicken Curry Noodles

khanom jeen kai

NUT-FREE This curry is a delightful red, but the bright hue is not from traditional red curry paste. Prepare this simple paste the night before you cook this dish, and add it along with the other ingredients to the slow cooker in the morning. Chicken legs hold up well to slow cooking, remaining juicy and plump; however, if you prefer, you can substitute breasts for the legs.

SERVES 4 TO 6
PREP TIME: 20 MINUTES
COOK TIME: 4 TO 6 HOURS ON LOW

FOR THE CURRY PASTE

2 teaspoons coriander seeds

10 pods green cardamom,
　　seeds removed from pods

4 dried California chiles, stemmed

⅓ cup diced shallots

⅓ cup diced fresh ginger

¼ cup diced turmeric root

1 cup coconut cream, divided

2 teaspoons curry powder

2 teaspoons salt

FOR THE CHICKEN AND NOODLES

2 cups water

8 chicken legs

¼ cup thin soy sauce

2 teaspoons palm sugar

1 (16-ounce) package angel hair pasta
　　or somen noodles

2 (13.5-ounce) cans coconut milk

¼ cup chopped fresh cilantro,
　　for garnish

¼ cup chopped scallions, for garnish

Lime wedges, for garnish

TO MAKE THE CURRY PASTE

1. In a dry skillet over medium heat, toast the coriander seeds and cardamom until fragrant. Transfer to a small bowl to cool.

2. Put the chiles in the bowl of a food processor. Add the shallots, ginger, turmeric, and cooled coriander and cardamom to the food processor bowl. Add ½ cup of coconut cream, and process until the mixture is smooth. Add the curry powder, salt, and remaining coconut cream, and process again to incorporate. Transfer the curry paste to the slow cooker.

TO MAKE THE CHICKEN AND NOODLES

1. Add the water, chicken legs, soy sauce, and palm sugar to the slow cooker. Cook on low for 4 to 6 hours.

2. Toward the end of cooking, bring a large pot of water to a boil and cook the noodles until tender.

3. Add the coconut milk to the curry, stirring to incorporate. Continue to cook until heated through, about 5 minutes.

4. Ladle the curry over the noodles. Garnish with the cilantro, scallions, and lime, and serve.

Cooking tip: Using California chiles produces a rather mild result. If you want a spicier curry, add one or two Thai chiles to the paste, or for the really bold, replace all the California chiles with Thai chiles. While Thai chiles are substantially smaller, they are much hotter.

Garbanzo Bean Red Curry Noodles ~ *khanom jeen*

NUT-FREE | QUICK PREP **This light, simple-to-make curry highlights how modest ingredients can easily be enlivened in Thai cooking. The spicy curry is thickened with puréed garbanzo beans, and like many Thai curries, made rich with coconut milk. Top the dish with the usual cohorts of Thai basil and bean sprouts, and you have a delightful mix of crisp accompaniments balancing the curry's succulent sauce.**

SERVES 4 TO 6
PREP TIME: 10 MINUTES
COOK TIME: 4 TO 6 HOURS ON LOW

2 cups cooked garbanzo beans

¾ cup Red Curry Paste (page 128) or store bought

½ teaspoon ground ginger

3 cups Vegetable Stock (page 119) or Chicken Stock (page 118), or store bought

¼ cup thin soy sauce

¼ cup palm sugar

1 (16-ounce) package angel hair pasta or somen noodles

2 (13.5-ounce) cans coconut milk

2 cups bean sprouts

1 cup fresh Thai basil

1. In a food processor, process the garbanzo beans until crumbly. Transfer to the slow cooker, and add the Red Curry Paste, ground ginger, Vegetable Stock, soy sauce, and palm sugar.

2. Cook on low for 4 to 6 hours.

3. Bring a large pot of water to a boil, and cook the noodles until tender. Rinse the noodles under cool water to remove excess starch.

4. Before serving, add the coconut milk to the curry and allow it to heat through, about 10 minutes.

5. Divide the noodles among plates, and ladle the curry over them. Garnish with bean sprouts and Thai basil, and serve.

Cooking tip: When serving Thai food, it is typical to add the garnishes at the table as you eat. When eating family style, arrange the garnish items on a large plate, and allow guests to grab as much as they choose to add flavor to their dish.

Crab Curry Noodles

khanom jeen nam ya pak tai

SOY-FREE | NUT-FREE | QUICK PREP In Thai cuisine, seafood is king, and there is no better king of the sea than the crab. Let your worries melt away as you savor this exquisite curry, a culinary transport to the sandy shores of faraway beaches. Served over noodles, this is another simple addition to your slow-cooking repertoire that will have you looking forward to dinner at home. Notice the short cooking time on this recipe—after a long day, just throw the ingredients in your slow cooker, boil some noodles, and in just an hour, you can unwind with a delicious meal.

SERVES 6

PREP TIME: 10 MINUTES

COOK TIME: 6 HOURS ON LOW,
1 HOUR ON HIGH

½ cup Yellow Curry Paste (page 132)
   or store bought

3 cups water

1 tablespoon palm sugar

¼ cup tamarind pulp

2 cans coconut milk

4 cups cooked lump crab meat

2 tablespoons fish sauce

1 (16-ounce) package angel hair
   pasta or somen noodles

Bean sprouts, for garnish

Hard-boiled eggs, for garnish

Thai basil, for garnish

1. In the slow cooker, stir together the Yellow Curry Paste, water, palm sugar, and tamarind pulp. Cook on high for 45 minutes, or on low for up to 6 hours.

2. Adjust the heat to high, and add the coconut milk, crab meat, and fish sauce. Replace the top, and continue to cook for 15 more minutes.

3. Bring a large pot of water to a boil, and immerse the noodles briefly to soften, about 3 to 5 minutes.

4. Divide the noodles among plates, and ladle the curry over them. Garnish with the bean sprouts, eggs, and basil, and serve.

Cooking tip: Hard-boiled eggs are a tough ingredient to master. For easy success, add cold eggs to a pot of water, and bring to a hard boil. Turn off the heat, cover the pot, and set a timer for 10 minutes. Avoid using fresh eggs, as they will be too hard to peel. If you are having trouble removing the shells, refrigerate the eggs after cooking to ease the process.

5

VEGETABLE DISHES

....

Green Mixed Vegetable Curry

kaeng khiew wan kap pak

NUT-FREE | QUICK PREP Green curry is a classic curry that translates well using any protein. Here, a mix of broccoli, baby corn, bell peppers, and tofu form the basis of this hot yet sweet dish. To make it vegetarian, make the Green Curry Paste yourself (page 129), omitting the shrimp paste, and choose Vegetable Stock (page 119) rather than chicken. Get creative and make this curry with a variety of your favorite vegetables—try it with beans, eggplant, squash, or others for your own unique blend. If you prefer, omit the tofu, and make it with just the vegetables for a satisfying, but lighter meal.

SERVES 4 TO 6
PREP TIME: 10 MINUTES
COOK TIME: 4 TO 6 HOURS ON LOW

1 cup Green Curry Paste (page 129)
  or store bought
1 cup Vegetable Stock (page 119)
  or Chicken Stock (page 118),
  or store bought
1½ cups broccoli florets
1 cup baby corn
1 cup sliced mushrooms
1 cup sliced (into strips) red or
  green bell pepper
¼ cup palm sugar
½ cup thin soy sauce
1 (13.5-ounce) can coconut milk
8 ounces firm tofu, diced
1 cup fresh Thai basil

1. In the slow cooker, stir together the Green Curry Paste and Vegetable Stock. Add the broccoli, baby corn, mushrooms, and bell peppers.

2. Chop the palm sugar into small pieces, and mix it into the slow cooker. Add the soy sauce.

3. Cook on low for 4 to 6 hours.

4. Add the coconut milk and tofu, and continue cooking until heated through, about 10 minutes.

5. Mix in the Thai basil, stirring until it wilts, about 1 minute. Serve.

Cooking tip: Commercial pastes are more concentrated and spicy than homemade pastes, so if you are using a store-bought paste and not making your own, reduce the amount of paste used. About ¼ cup of commercial green curry paste will provide enough spice and flavor in this dish.

Massaman Sweet Potato and Tofu Curry

This mild curry transforms otherwise ordinary sweet potatoes into delectable morsels of goodness. Adding pan-fried tofu creates a winning texture as this saucy curry holds onto individual bite-size pieces with ease. The addition of tofu and peanuts provides protein in a dish that's simple to get started in the slow cooker on a busy morning. To make the dish vegetarian, use Vegetable Stock (page 119), and swap out the shrimp paste for an additional ¼ teaspoon of salt when making the Massaman Curry Paste (page 130).

SERVES 4 TO 6
PREP TIME: 15 MINUTES
COOK TIME: 4 TO 6 HOURS ON LOW

2 medium sweet potatoes

1 cup Massaman Curry Paste (page 130) or store bought

2 cups Vegetable Stock (page 119) or Chicken Stock (page 118), or store bought

4 tablespoons palm sugar

4 tablespoons thin soy sauce

3 tablespoons vegetable oil

8 ounces firm tofu, diced into 1-inch cubes

1 (13.5-ounce) can coconut milk

⅔ cup roasted, unsalted peanuts

1. In the slow cooker, stir together the sweet potatoes, Massaman Curry Paste, Vegetable Stock, palm sugar, and soy sauce.

2. Cook on low for 4 to 6 hours.

3. In a large skillet, heat the vegetable oil over medium-high heat. Dry the tofu squares well with a clean kitchen towel. Add the pieces to the pan, cooking for about 3 minutes on each side, until browned. Remove and drain on paper towels.

4. Add the tofu squares, coconut milk, and peanuts to the slow cooker, stirring to combine. Cook for an additional 10 minutes to heat through, and serve with jasmine rice.

Cooking tip: If you prefer to skip pan-frying the tofu yourself, look for fried tofu squares at the grocery store. Typically positioned in the cold section near traditional tofu, pre-fried tofu squares can cut down your prep time when making this dish, and they cost little more than fresh tofu.

Vegetable Red Curry with Cashews

SOY-FREE | QUICK PREP Cashews add a desirable crunchiness to this spicy, savory curry. Red curry shines with a combination of cauliflower, sweet potatoes, peas, and mushrooms, providing a filling meal with little effort. If using a store-bought curry paste rather than making your own, be sure to scale back, if you prefer your end result less than red-hot.

SERVES 4 TO 6
PREP TIME: 10 MINUTES
COOK TIME: 4 TO 6 HOURS ON LOW

1 head cauliflower, cut into florets

2 sweet potatoes, diced into
   1-inch chunks

1 onion, diced

¾ cup Red Curry Paste (page 128)
   or store bought

1 cup Vegetable Stock (page 119)
   or Chicken Stock (page 118),
   or store bought

1 tablespoon palm sugar

1 (13.5-ounce) can coconut milk

1 cup sliced white mushrooms

1 cup green peas

½ cup cashews

¼ cup chopped fresh cilantro

¼ cup Thai basil leaves

1. In the slow cooker, stir together the cauliflower, sweet potatoes, onion, Red Curry Paste, Vegetable Stock, and palm sugar.

2. Cook on low for 4 to 6 hours.

3. Add the coconut milk, mushrooms, and peas, and cook for 30 more minutes.

4. Preheat the oven to 350°F.

5. Spread the cashews on a baking sheet, and put them in the oven to toast for 7 to 10 minutes.

6. Ladle the curry into a serving bowl, and top with the cashews, cilantro, and basil. Serve with jasmine rice.

Vegetarian Jungle Curry

kaeng pha pak

NUT-FREE | QUICK PREP   This saucy curry is just the thing for a lover of spice. Made without coconut milk, there is no forgiving sweetness to jungle curry. Instead, this intensely flavored herbal curry makes ample use of aromatics to enliven its flavor. To keep this dish vegetarian, omit the shrimp paste when preparing the paste (page 133). If you don't have access to yard-long beans, substitute fresh green beans instead.

SERVES 6
PREP TIME: 10 MINUTES
COOK TIME: 4 TO 6 HOURS ON LOW

1 cup Jungle Curry Paste (page 133)
   or store bought
4 cups Vegetable Stock (page 119),
   or store bought
2 cups baby corn
2 cups yard-long beans, cut into
   1-inch segments
1 cup cherry tomatoes, halved
1½ cups sliced shiitake mushrooms
¼ cup palm sugar
6 tablespoons thin soy sauce
1 cup chopped fresh sage
1 cup Thai basil leaves

1. In the slow cooker, stir together the Jungle Curry Paste, Vegetable Stock, baby corn, beans, tomatoes, mushrooms, palm sugar, and soy sauce.

2. Cook on low for 4 to 6 hours.

3. In the last 5 minutes of cooking, add the sage and Thai basil, stirring until they wilt. Serve over jasmine rice.

Yellow Vegetable and Tofu Curry

NUT-FREE | QUICK PREP By the time you eat this curry, the vegetables will be falling-apart tender, and the sweet, turmeric-laced curry will have infused all in its path. Use this blend of vegetables, or choose your own favorites to make this mild curry shine. To make the curry vegetarian, omit the shrimp paste in the Yellow Curry Paste (page 132), and use Vegetable Stock (page 119).

SERVES 6
PREP TIME: 10 MINUTES
COOK TIME: 4 TO 6 HOURS ON LOW

1 cup Yellow Curry Paste (page 132)
   or store bought
2 cups Vegetable Stock (page 119)
   or Chicken Stock (page 118),
   or store bought
1 head cauliflower, cut into florets
2 medium Yukon Gold or red potatoes
1 cup baby corn
1 red or green bell pepper,
   cut into strips
1 (13.5-ounce) can coconut milk
8 ounces firm tofu, cut into small cubes
1 cup loosely packed Thai basil leaves

1. In the slow cooker, stir together the Yellow Curry Paste, Vegetable Stock, cauliflower, potatoes, baby corn, and bell pepper.

2. Cook on low for 4 to 6 hours.

3. Stir in the coconut milk and tofu, and continue to cook for 10 minutes, until heated through.

4. Add the Thai basil, and stir until just wilted, about 1 minute. Serve with jasmine rice.

Sweet and Sour Vegetables

phad prio wan phak

NUT-FREE | QUICK PREP   There is a common misconception that all Thai food is spicy. It's true that many signature dishes are known for their intense heat, but in fact, several lesser-known dishes have no spice at all. This is one of those dishes. Popular in northern Thailand, this simple vegetable dish is flavored with a combination of lime juice, fish sauce, soy sauce, and tamarind water.

SERVES 4 TO 6
PREP TIME: 10 MINUTES
COOK TIME: 4 TO 6 HOURS ON LOW

1 large onion, sliced

1 head cauliflower, cut into florets

2 carrots, peeled and sliced

2 cups baby corn

2 cups diced pineapple

2 tomatoes, diced

1 cup Chicken Stock (page 118)
   or Vegetable Stock (page 119),
   or store bought

¼ cup sugar

¼ cup freshly squeezed lime juice

3 tablespoons fish sauce

3 tablespoons thin soy sauce

6 tablespoons Tamarind Water
   (page 124)

1 cup snow peas

1. In the slow cooker, stir together the onion, cauliflower, carrots, baby corn, pineapple, and tomatoes.

2. In a small bowl, stir together the Chicken Stock, sugar, lime juice, fish sauce, soy sauce, and Tamarind Water, and pour into the slow cooker.

3. Cook on low for 4 to 6 hours.

4. About 30 minutes before serving, add the snow peas. Serve over jasmine rice.

Cooking tip: Because this dish lacks spice, it provides an excellent cooling contrast to a spicier item. Try serving it with Papaya Salad (page 104) or a spicy jungle curry.

6

SEAFOOD DISHES

....

Shrimp and Scallop Red Curry

kaeng phed hoi cheo kung

SOY-FREE | NUT-FREE | QUICK PREP Thailand is known for its seafood, and this red curry showcases three of the most flavorful offerings: shrimp, clams, and scallops. Cook the curry and vegetables during the day, and finish the dish by quick-sautéing the shrimp and scallops, adding them to the curry at the end to retain their tender texture. If using a commercially prepared curry paste, make sure to scale back to keep the spice level in check.

SERVES 4 TO 6
PREP TIME: 10 MINUTES
COOK TIME: 6 TO 8 HOURS ON LOW,
3 TO 5 HOURS ON HIGH

¾ cup Red Curry Paste (page 128)
    or store bought
2 cups baby corn
1 red bell pepper, cut into strips
2 onions, chopped
2 cups Chicken Stock (page 118)
    or Vegetable Stock (page 119),
    or store bought
1 (13.5-ounce) can coconut milk,
    refrigerated and divided
1 pound littleneck clams, washed
    several times until water runs clear
1 pound sea scallops
1 pound large shrimp,
    peeled and deveined
Juice of 2 key limes
2 tablespoons oyster sauce
2 cups loosely packed Thai basil leaves

1. In the slow cooker, stir together the Red Curry Paste, baby corn, bell pepper, onions, and Chicken Stock. Cook on low for 6 to 8 hours, or high for 3 to 5 hours.

2. Open the can of chilled coconut milk (without shaking it), and scrape 2 tablespoons of the coconut cream from its surface. In a large skillet, bring the coconut cream and about 2 tablespoons of the coconut water from the can to a simmer, and add the clams. Cover the skillet, and simmer for another 5 to 7 minutes, or until the clams open. Discard any that do not. Using a slotted spoon, transfer the clams to the slow cooker.

3. Add the scallops and shrimp to the pan, sautéing until they are just cooked through. Add them, along with the coconut cream, to the slow cooker.

4. Add the lime juice, oyster sauce, Thai basil, and remaining coconut milk and cream to the slow cooker, and cook until heated through, about 5 minutes.

5. Serve with jasmine rice.

Ingredient tip: Thai basil can wilt rather quickly once you get it home. To extend its shelf life, keep it out of the refrigerator, which quickly deteriorates its quality. Instead, store it on the counter with its cut ends submerged in a glass of water.

White Fish Green Curry

kaeng kieow wan plaa

SOY-FREE | NUT-FREE | QUICK PREP   White fish is the perfect protein in a curry, as it holds its texture well and creates a lighter result than curries made with meats. Simmer the sauce slowly throughout the day, and add the fish at the end of cooking to enjoy this simple meal with little fuss. As always, if using a store-bought curry paste, remember to reduce the quantity to avoid over-spicing your dish.

SERVES 4 TO 6
PREP TIME: 10 MINUTES
COOK TIME: 6 HOURS ON LOW,
PLUS 30 MINUTES ON HIGH

2 cups Vegetable Stock (page 119)
    or Chicken Stock (page 118),
    or store bought
1 cup Green Curry Paste (page 129)
    or store bought
2 tablespoons fish sauce
2 tablespoons palm sugar
2 cups bamboo shoots
1 red bell pepper, cut into strips
2 pounds filleted white fish (tilapia,
    sole, cod), cut into bite-size pieces
2 cups green peas
2 cups coconut milk
½ cup loosely packed Thai basil leaves

1. In the slow cooker, stir together the Vegetable Stock, Green Curry Paste, fish sauce, palm sugar, bamboo shoots, and bell pepper.

2. Cook on low for 6 hours.

3. The adjust the slow cooker to high. Add the fish, peas, and coconut milk, and cook for 30 additional minutes.

4. Add the Thai basil, and stir until lightly wilted, about 1 minute. Adjust the seasoning as needed, adding more fish sauce or palm sugar according to preference.

5. Serve with jasmine rice.

Cooking tip: Be sure to defrost the fish for this curry before leaving the house in the morning so you can quickly finish it on your return. Fish should be thawed in the refrigerator. Simply transfer the needed amount to a plate, and refrigerate until ready to use.

White Fish and Kabocha Red Curry

kaeng phed plaa

SOY-FREE | NUT-FREE Red curry provides a warming comfort on a cool day. Here, when combined with a sturdy white fish, it's a nourishing meal that is perfect for lunch or dinner. As with many curries, the flavors improve after a day or two of refrigeration, so be sure to save your leftovers for a lunch later in the week. If you opt for store-bought curry paste rather than making your own, don't forget to use less—or be prepared for some bold heat.

SERVES 4 TO 6
PREP TIME: 15 MINUTES
COOK TIME: 6 HOURS ON LOW,
PLUS 30 MINUTES ON HIGH

1 pound kabocha, cored, and cut into 1-inch chunks, and peeled

2 cups Chicken Stock (page 118) or Vegetable Stock (page 119), or store bought

¾ cup Red Curry Paste (page 128) or store bought

2 tablespoons fish sauce

3 tablespoons palm sugar

1½ pounds firm white fish (tilapia, sole, cod), cut into bite-size pieces

1 (13.5-ounce) can coconut milk

1 cup loosely packed Thai basil leaves

1. In the slow cooker, stir together the kabocha, Chicken Stock, Red Curry Paste, fish sauce, and palm sugar.

2. Cook on low for 6 hours.

3. Then adjust the slow cooker to high. Add the fish to the slow cooker along with the coconut milk. Cover and cook for 30 more minutes.

4. Add the Thai basil, stirring until wilted, 1 to 2 minutes. Season with additional palm sugar or fish sauce as desired.

5. Serve with jasmine rice.

Ingredient tip: Cutting a kabocha can be tricky, so be sure your knife is properly sharpened before you begin. First, slice the kabocha in half by inserting the knife tip below the stem and working it downward. Use a sturdy spoon to remove the seeds, and if you like, reserve them for roasting. Cut the kabocha halves into strips, and those into chunks. Once you crack the squash open, you'll find it easier to handle. If available, purchase a precut kabocha in the refrigerated section of many Asian markets and grocery stores.

Salmon Red Curry

SOY-FREE | NUT-FREE | QUICK PREP Salmon is not a native fish to Thailand, but it still pairs well with the flavors of Thai cooking. Here, beans, baby corn, and red bell pepper form a colorful backdrop for this saucy curry that enlivens the senses. Create the sauce in your slow cooker while you are out for the day, then come home and add the fillets to finish the meal. To keep the spice level from rising extra high, be sure to cut down on curry paste if using premade.

SERVES 4 TO 6
PREP TIME: 10 MINUTES
COOK TIME: 6 HOURS ON LOW,
PLUS 30 MINUTES ON HIGH

¾ cup Red Curry Paste (page 128)
   or store bought
2 cups Chicken Stock (page 118)
   or Vegetable Stock (page 119),
   or store bought
1 cup yard-long beans
1 cup baby corn
1 red bell pepper, cut into strips
1½ pounds salmon fillets
1 (13.5-ounce) can coconut milk
1 tablespoon palm sugar
2 tablespoons fish sauce
1 cup loosely packed Thai basil leaves

1. In the slow cooker, stir together the Red Curry Paste, Chicken Stock, yard-long beans, baby corn, and red bell pepper strips.

2. Cook on low for 6 hours.

3. Then adjust the slow cooker to high. Add the salmon and coconut milk, and cook for an additional 30 minutes, or until the fish flakes.

4. Add the palm sugar and fish sauce. Adjust the flavors as needed, adding more fish sauce or palm sugar as desired. Stir in the basil leaves, and continue to stir until they are wilted, about 1 minute.

5. Serve with jasmine rice or rice noodles.

Cooking tip: This curry provides a nice, simple solution for making use of leftover salmon. To do this, instead of adjusting the slow cooker to high at the end, simply add the precooked salmon and coconut milk, and continue to cook for 10 more minutes until heated through. Mix in the basil and serve.

Salmon and Shrimp Jungle Curry

kaeng paa moo plaa kung

SOY-FREE | NUT-FREE | QUICK PREP   Jungle curry is infamously spicy, and this slow cooker favorite is no exception. Salmon and shrimp are the standouts in this saucy dish that is not for the faint of heart. To better control heat, consider making the Jungle Curry Paste yourself (page 133) and crafting it to suit your desired heat level, while still getting plenty of the herbaceous blend that makes it so unique.

SERVES 6

PREP TIME: 10 MINUTES

COOK TIME: 6 TO 8 HOURS ON LOW, PLUS 30 MINUTES ON HIGH

3 cups Chicken Stock (page 118) or Vegetable Stock (page 119), or store bought

1 cup Jungle Curry Paste (page 133) or store bought

1 cup bamboo shoots

2 tablespoons fish sauce

1 tablespoon palm sugar

2 salmon fillets

1 pound large shrimp, peeled and deveined

1 cup loosely packed Thai basil leaves

1 cup chopped chives

1. In the slow cooker, stir together the Chicken Stock, Jungle Curry Paste, bamboo shoots, fish sauce, and palm sugar.

2. Cook on low for 6 to 8 hours.

3. Adjust the heat to high, and add the salmon fillets and shrimp. Cook for 30 more minutes, or until the fish flakes and the shrimp are cooked through.

4. Garnish with the Thai basil and chopped chives, and serve with jasmine rice.

Seafood and Kabocha Yellow Curry *kaeng karii*

SOY-FREE | NUT-FREE | QUICK PREP Seafood pairs wonderfully with yellow curry to create a mild yet grown-up dish. Use the suggested mussels, shrimp, white fish, and calamari combination, or substitute your favorite seafood in this sweet curry. Start cooking the curry and kabocha in the morning; then add the seafood after a long slow-cooking session to complete this simple-to-make, outrageously delicious meal.

SERVES 4 TO 6
PREP TIME: 10 MINUTES
COOK TIME: 6½ TO 8½ HOURS ON LOW,
3½ TO 5½ HOURS ON HIGH

1 cup Yellow Curry Paste (page 132),
  or store bought
2 cups Chicken Stock (page 118)
  or Vegetable Stock (page 119),
  or store bought
1 pound kabocha, peeled, cored,
  and diced
½ pound large shrimp,
  peeled and deveined
½ pound mussels, beards removed
  and cleaned
½ pound firm white fish (tilapia, sole,
  cod), cut into bite-size pieces
½ pound calamari
1 (13.5-ounce) can coconut milk
1 tablespoon palm sugar
2 tablespoons fish sauce
½ cup roughly chopped cilantro leaves

1. In the slow cooker, stir together the Yellow Curry Paste, Chicken Stock, and kabocha.

2. Cook on low for 6 to 8 hours, or on high for 3 to 5 hours.

3. If cooking on low, adjust the slow cooker to high. Add the shrimp, mussels, fish, and calamari, stirring to combine. Pour the coconut milk over the top, and stir again. Cook for an additional 30 minutes.

4. Add the palm sugar and fish sauce. Adjust the seasonings as needed, adding more fish sauce or palm sugar if desired.

5. Stir in the cilantro leaves, and serve over jasmine rice.

7

CHICKEN DISHES

....

Chicken Yellow Curry

kaeng karii gai

SOY-FREE | NUT-FREE | QUICK PREP   A mild, crowd-pleasing favorite, yellow curry is a versatile addition to your slow cooker repertoire. While traditional yellow curry rarely includes more than chicken and potatoes, here the dish is enlivened with a medley of vegetables to add both color and flavor to the warming curry. Use the vegetables noted, or substitute your favorites in equal proportion for a meal suited to your tastes.

SERVES 4 TO 6

PREP TIME: 10 MINUTES

COOK TIME: 4½ TO 6½ HOURS ON LOW

1 cup Yellow Curry Paste (page 132) or store bought

1½ cups Chicken Stock (page 118) or store bought

1½ pounds boneless chicken breasts, thighs, or a combination, diced

1 pound Yukon Gold or red potatoes, cut into 2-inch cubes

1 cup sliced mushrooms

1 red bell pepper, cut into strips

1 cup broccoli florets

¼ cup fish sauce

2 tablespoons palm sugar

1 (13.5-ounce) can coconut milk

1 small zucchini, sliced

½ cup loosely packed Thai basil leaves, plus more for garnish

1. In the slow cooker, stir together the Yellow Curry Paste, Chicken Stock, chicken, potatoes, mushrooms, bell pepper, broccoli florets, fish sauce, and palm sugar.

2. Cook on low for 4 to 6 hours.

3. Add the coconut milk and zucchini, and cook for an additional 30 minutes.

4. Adjust the seasonings as desired, adding more fish sauce or palm sugar as needed. Add the Thai basil leaves, stirring until they wilt. Garnish with a couple of additional torn or shredded Thai basil leaves.

5. Serve over jasmine rice.

Chicken Green Curry ✺ *kaeng kieow wan gai*

SOY-FREE | NUT-FREE | QUICK PREP Eggplant is an under-utilized ingredient in the West. In Thailand, on the other hand, it is widely used in green curry, as it pairs well with spice to provide cooling. To prepare this curry, look for Thai eggplants, the circular green variety, as they are exceptionally delicious in this recipe. Prep the chicken the night before to make this quick mix-and-go curry the next morning, or leave the breasts whole and shred them just before serving. As always, you can make your own curry paste or buy one commercially prepared—if the latter, just remember to cut back.

SERVES 4 TO 6
PREP TIME: 10 MINUTES
COOK TIME: 6½ HOURS ON LOW

1 cup Green Curry Paste (page 129)
    or store bought
1½ cups Chicken Stock (page 118)
    or store bought
1½ pounds boneless chicken breasts,
    thighs, or a combination, diced
¼ cup fish sauce
2 tablespoons palm sugar
1 (13.5-ounce) can coconut milk
8 Thai eggplants, quartered
½ cup loosely packed Thai basil leaves

1. In the slow cooker, stir together the Green Curry Paste, Chicken Stock, chicken, fish sauce, and palm sugar.

2. Cook on low for 6 hours.

3. Add the coconut milk and eggplant, and cook for an additional 30 minutes.

4. Adjust the seasonings as desired, adding more fish sauce or palm sugar as needed. Add the Thai basil leaves, stirring until they wilt.

5. Serve over jasmine rice.

Ingredient tip: If you can't find Thai eggplants, substitute slender Japanese or Chinese eggplants in their place. These tend to be moister than Thai eggplants, so before adding them to the curry, soak them for 5 minutes in a bowl containing 2 teaspoons of salt mixed with 1 quart of water. This simple trick will extract some of the moisture.

Chicken Red Curry

kaeng phed gai

SOY-FREE | NUT-FREE | QUICK PREP Red curry is often prepared with bamboo shoots, whose cool texture and mild flavor pairs well with the spice of this bright, spicy curry. In Southeast Asia bamboo shoots are plentiful after the rainy season, but in the Western world, they are most widely available canned. For those interested, you may be able to find fresh bamboo shoots in an Asian market in winter, but for quick prep, canned is the way to go. If using a premade curry paste, be sure to add a much smaller quantity—or you might singe your guests with spice!

SERVES 4 TO 6
PREP TIME: 10 MINUTES
COOK TIME: 4 TO 6 HOURS ON LOW

¾ cup Red Curry Paste (page 128) or store bought

1 pound boneless, skinless chicken breasts, thighs, or a combination, cut into cubes

1 cup Chicken Stock (page 118) or store bought

1 (8-ounce) can bamboo shoots

3 tablespoons palm sugar

2 tablespoons fish sauce

1 (13.5-ounce) can coconut milk

1 cup loosely packed Thai basil

1. In the slow cooker, stir together the Red Curry Paste, chicken, Chicken Stock, bamboo shoots, palm sugar, and fish sauce.

2. Cook on low for 4 to 6 hours.

3. Add the coconut milk to the curry, and cook for an additional 10 minutes to heat through.

4. Adjust the seasonings, adding more palm sugar or fish sauce as desired. Add the Thai basil, stirring until it wilts.

5. Serve over jasmine rice.

Chicken Jungle Curry

kaeng pa gai

SOY-FREE | NUT-FREE | QUICK PREP **Native to northern Thailand, where coconuts do not grow, this curry was developed based on locally available ingredients. With chicken, the thin curry is mouthwateringly spicy, making the pairing with baby corn, bamboo shoots, and mushrooms a cooling contrast. Prep the chicken the night before to eliminate work in the morning, and you'll have this ready for your slow cooker in no time.**

SERVES 4 TO 6

PREP TIME: 10 MINUTES

COOK TIME: 4 TO 6 HOURS ON LOW

1 pound chicken breasts, thighs, or a combination, diced

3 cups Chicken Stock (page 118) or store bought

1 cup Jungle Curry Paste (page 133) or store bought

1 cup bamboo shoots

1 cup baby corn

1 cup straw mushrooms

1 cup yard-long beans, cut into 1-inch segments

2 tablespoons fish sauce

1 tablespoon palm sugar

¾ cup loosely packed, torn Thai basil leaves

1. In the slow cooker, stir together the chicken, Chicken Stock, Jungle Curry Paste, bamboo shoots, baby corn, mushrooms, beans, fish sauce, and palm sugar.

2. Cook on low for 4 to 6 hours.

3. Adjust the seasonings if needed, adding more fish sauce or palm sugar.

4. Stir in the Thai basil, and continue stirring until the leaves are wilted.

5. Serve over jasmine rice.

Cooking tip: To best control the spice in a jungle curry, make the paste yourself. One of the few non-coconut-based curries, jungle curry is highly aromatic and complex. Because of its biting heat, many people stay away from this one, but don't let its spicy reputation stop you. Rather, opt for mild California peppers or a mix of spicy and mild peppers to ensure the paste is suited to your palate.

Chicken Penang Curry

kaeng penang gai

SOY-FREE | NUT-FREE | QUICK PREP Penang curry is a touch milder than many of the other Thai curries in this book, making it a good choice for a dinner party with a diverse guest list. Traditionally made with beef or even water buffalo, the dish is slightly lighter with chicken. For quick prep in the morning, dice the chicken the night before, and you can have this cooking in less than 10 minutes in the morning.

SERVES 4 TO 6
PREP TIME: 10 MINUTES
COOK TIME: 4 TO 6 HOURS ON LOW

¾ cup Penang Curry Paste (page 131) or store bought

1 cup Chicken Stock (page 118) or store bought

1 pound chicken breasts, thighs, or a combination, diced

1 red bell pepper, cut into strips

2 tablespoons fish sauce

1 tablespoon palm sugar

1 (13.5-ounce) can coconut milk

½ cup torn sweet basil leaves

1. In the slow cooker, stir together the Penang Curry Paste, Chicken Stock, chicken, bell pepper, fish sauce, and palm sugar.

2. Cook on low for 4 to 6 hours.

3. Add the coconut milk, and cook for an additional 10 minutes to heat through.

4. Adjust the seasonings as desired, adding more fish sauce or palm sugar as needed.

5. Add the basil leaves, and stir until wilted, about 1 minute.

6. Serve with jasmine rice.

Chicken Massaman Curry

kaeng masamun gai

SOY-FREE   Using a whole chicken, this recipe is a crowd-pleasing favorite. Searing the chicken helps lock in flavor during the slow-cooking process—an especially important step for leaner cuts of meat. The addition of peanuts gives a lively texture to the finished product, while coconut provides a soothing creaminess.

SERVES 4 TO 6
PREP TIME: 20 MINUTES
COOK TIME: 4 TO 6 HOURS ON LOW

4 medium Yukon Gold or red
   potatoes, diced
2 cups Chicken Stock (page 118)
   or store bought
1 cup Massaman Curry Paste
   (page 130) or store bought
2 red onions, sliced
⅓ cup fish sauce
¼ cup freshly squeezed lime juice
2 tablespoons palm sugar
2 tablespoons vegetable oil
1 whole chicken, cut into 10 pieces
Kosher salt
1 (13.5-ounce) can coconut milk
½ cup ground, dry-roasted peanuts

1. In the slow cooker, stir together the potatoes, Chicken Stock, Massaman Curry Paste, onions, fish sauce, lime juice, and palm sugar.

2. In a Dutch oven, heat the oil until shimmering. Sprinkle the chicken with salt, and add several pieces to the pot. Sear each side until just browned, and transfer to the slow cooker. Continue until all the pieces are browned.

3. Cook on low for 4 to 6 hours.

4. Add the coconut milk and peanuts to the slow cooker, and continue to cook for 10 minutes, until heated through. Adjust the seasonings as desired by adding more fish sauce or palm sugar.

5. Serve with jasmine rice.

Cooking tip: Cutting up a chicken is an inexpensive way to make a meal for several people. Remove the legs and wings first, followed by the thighs, cutting between the bones to dislodge the pieces. Remove the back of the chicken with kitchen shears. Split the breast into two sides, then cut each breast in half. Save the back of the chicken in the freezer for the next time you make Chicken Stock.

Thai Chicken Salad ~ *larb*

SOY-FREE | NUT-FREE A Northern Thai specialty, *larb* is a classic dish. Served both hot and cooled, this salad can accompany rice or be served with fresh lettuce leaves to scoop up the spicy minced meat. Be mindful that the chili powder in this recipe is not the blend of spices used to season tacos and other Mexican foods, but ground Thai chili powder.

SERVES 4 TO 6
PREP TIME: 15 MINUTES
COOK TIME: 4 TO 6 HOURS ON LOW

1 pound ground chicken

¼ cup thinly sliced lemongrass

¾ cup sliced shallots

4 tablespoons roasted rice powder
   (see Cooking tip)

½ cup loosely packed, sliced
   cilantro leaves

½ cup loosely packed, sliced
   mint leaves

¼ cup freshly squeezed lime juice

2 tablespoons fish sauce

2 teaspoons dried Thai chili powder

1 teaspoon white sugar

1 cup water

1. In the slow cooker, mix together the chicken, lemongrass, shallots, rice powder, cilantro, mint, lime juice, fish sauce, chili powder, sugar, and water, using your hands to mix it uniformly. Do not pack the meat down, but instead leave it crumbly in the liner.

2. Cook on low for 4 to 6 hours.

3. At the end of cooking, remove the lid, and continue to cook for 10 minutes, or until most of the liquid has evaporated.

4. Serve with jasmine rice.

Cooking tip: To make roasted rice powder, dry roast jasmine rice in a skillet until it is lightly browned. Grind the rice in a mortar, or process it in a spice grinder, until it becomes powder.

Chicken with Leeks

kai phat tom hom yai

SOY-FREE | NUT-FREE | QUICK PREP The common perception of spicy Thai food is dispelled here with this simple dish popping with flavor. Leeks are the star of the show, their subtle flavor exuding into the meat. Completely free of chile peppers, this is a great recipe to pair with spicier dishes, like a hot soup or salad.

SERVES 4 TO 6
PREP TIME: 10 MINUTES
COOK TIME: 4 TO 6 HOURS ON LOW

1½ pounds bone-in chicken thighs, skin removed
1 cup Chicken Stock (page 118) or store bought
1 pound leeks, cleaned (see Ingredient tip) and sliced
10 crushed garlic cloves
4 tablespoons palm sugar
¼ cup fish sauce
¼ cup yellow bean sauce

Ingredient tip: Very similar in appearance to a giant scallion, leeks are a well-suited seasoning for a variety of dishes. Because they have multiple layers, however, dirt can easily get lodged inside. Therefore, before using, remove the outer layers and slice the leek in half lengthwise to clean out any dirt from the inner layers.

1. In the slow cooker, stir together the chicken thighs, Chicken Stock, leeks, garlic, palm sugar, fish sauce, and yellow bean sauce.

2. Cook on low for 4 to 6 hours.

3. Serve over jasmine rice.

Chicken in Red Chili and Cashews

kai phat met ma muang

SOY-FREE | QUICK PREP With close ties to Chinese cooking, this dish is just one of many Thai meals that demonstrate a strong influence from its neighbor to the north. Traditionally this dish is stir-fried, but it works just as well in the slow cooker to infuse the flavors that make it uniquely Thai. Chicken thighs are used to maximize juiciness over a lengthy cooking time.

SERVES 4
PREP TIME: 10 MINUTES
COOK TIME: 4 TO 6 HOURS ON LOW

1 pound boneless, skinless
   chicken thighs
¾ cup Chicken Stock (page 118)
   or store bought
1 onion, halved and sliced
10 garlic cloves, crushed and chopped
1 tablespoon Chile-Tamarind Paste
   (page 125) or store bought
1 tablespoon oyster sauce
1 tablespoon fish sauce
2 tablespoons palm sugar
1 cup roasted cashews
5 scallions, cut into 1-inch segments

1. In the slow cooker, stir together the chicken thighs, Chicken Stock, onion, garlic, Chili-Tamarind Paste, oyster sauce, fish sauce, and palm sugar.

2. Cook on low for 4 to 6 hours.

3. Mix in the cashews and scallions, and continue to cook for 10 more minutes.

4. Serve with jasmine rice.

Slow Cooker "Roasted" Hens

SOY-FREE | NUT-FREE   The Issan region of Thailand is known for its incredible roasted chickens. Cooked over a spit to allow for constant rotation, the end product is a bird that boasts juicy flesh, a golden coating, and unbeatable aroma. The secret to a crisp bird in the slow cooker is to lift it from the bottom of the cooker, so it doesn't stew in its own juices and become soggy. Finishing the hens briefly under the broiler gives them a crisp, browned coating.

SERVES 4 TO 6
PREP TIME: 20 MINUTES, PLUS
OVERNIGHT TO REST
COOK TIME: 4 TO 6 HOURS ON LOW

FOR THE BRINE

½ cup kosher salt

¼ cup sugar

8 cups water

1 teaspoon white peppercorns

1 stalk lemongrass, outer leaves and tough top removed, bottom trimmed, cut into 2-inch segments

3 garlic cloves, crushed

2 Cornish game hens

FOR THE STUFFING

2 stalks lemongrass, outer leaves and tough top removed, bottom trimmed, thinly sliced

½ cup halved garlic cloves

2 teaspoons kosher salt

1 teaspoon freshly ground white pepper

FOR THE MARINADE

2 teaspoons thick soy sauce

1 tablespoon fish sauce

1 teaspoon sugar

¼ teaspoon freshly ground black pepper

FOR THE BASTING SOLUTION

2 tablespoons honey

1 tablespoon warm water

TO MAKE AND USE THE BRINE

1. The night before, in a bowl large enough to contain the hens, stir together the salt, sugar, water, white peppercorns, lemongrass, and garlic, dissolving the sugar and salt.

2. Add the Cornish game hens , making sure they are submerged in the brine. Cover the bowl, and refrigerate.

TO MAKE THE STUFFING

1. In a medium bowl, stir together the lemongrass, garlic, salt, and pepper.

2. Refrigerate until ready for use.   >>

Slow Cooker "Roasted" Hens

TO MAKE THE MARINADE

In a small bowl, stir together the soy sauce, fish sauce, sugar, and pepper.

TO MAKE THE BASTING SOLUTION

In a small bowl, mix together the honey and water.

TO "ROAST" THE HENS

1. Remove the hens from the brine, allowing them to briefly drip dry.

2. Tear 5 square sheets of aluminum foil, and crumple them into balls. Place these in the bottom of the slow cooker.

3. Stuff the birds with the stuffing.

4. Using a brush, apply the marinade to the surface of the birds. Place the birds snugly in the slow cooker in opposite directions. In a circular cooker, they will touch, while in an oval one, there will be a little more room.

5. Cook on low for 4 to 6 hours.

6. Preheat the broiler.

7. Using tongs, remove the birds from the slow cooker carefully. Place them on a baking sheet, and brush the basting solution over them. Place them under the broiler for 5 to 7 minutes, turning the tray once during this time for uniform browning.

8. To serve, cut the hens in half lengthwise, then again across the breast to create four equal portions with each bird.

9. Serve the hens with Sweet-Spicy Chile Dipping Sauce (page 122) for the best flavor.

Thai Sticky Wings ✨

While not a traditional Thai recipe, sticky wings are loaded with Thai flavors for a finger-licking good meal. Cooking the wings in the slow cooker renders their fat nicely, leaving you with tender, juicy wings, but without all the fat. Finish the wings under a broiler to crisp up their exterior and lock on the sticky coating that makes them so lip-smackingly addictive.

SERVES 4 TO 6
PREP TIME: 15 MINUTES
COOK TIME: 4 HOURS ON LOW

4 pounds chicken wings, split, wing tips discarded
Salt
Freshly ground black pepper
½ cup thin soy sauce, divided
½ cup packed brown sugar, divided
4 tablespoons minced ginger, divided
2 tablespoons white vinegar
½ teaspoon dried chili powder
2 tablespoons freshly squeezed lime juice
¼ cup water
½ cup chopped peanuts
½ cup chopped fresh cilantro

1. Place the chicken wings in the slow cooker, and season them well with salt and pepper.

2. In a small bowl, stir together ¼ cup of soy sauce, ¼ cup of brown sugar, and 2 tablespoons of ginger. Add the mixture to the slow cooker, and stir together with the chicken wings.

3. Cook on low for 4 hours.

4. In a small saucepan, stir together the remaining ¼ cup of soy sauce, ¼ cup of brown sugar, and 2 tablespoons of ginger with the vinegar, chili powder, lime juice, and water. Bring to a boil, and turn down the heat to simmer until reduced by half, about 10 minutes.

5. Preheat the broiler.

6. Toss the wings in the sauce, and place them on a baking sheet and under the broiler for 8 minutes, flipping halfway through. Remove when they are crisp and browned.

7. Toss with the peanuts and cilantro, and serve.

8

MEAT DISHES

....

Beef Yellow Curry

kaeng karii neua

SOY-FREE | NUT-FREE | QUICK PREP   Yellow curry is famous for its mild spice level, which makes it especially suitable for children. Prepare the beef, onions, potatoes, and curry paste the night before, and store them all in the refrigerator until morning. Add them to the slow cooker with water, and you are well on your way to a delicious meal when you return home.

SERVES 4 TO 6
PREP TIME: 10 MINUTES
COOK TIME: 6 TO 8 HOURS ON LOW,
5 TO 7 HOURS ON HIGH

1½ pounds beef chuck, cut into
    2-inch cubes
1 cup Yellow Curry Paste (page 132)
    or store bought
1 pound Yukon Gold or red potatoes,
    cut into 2-inch cubes
2 medium onions, halved and sliced
¼ cup fish sauce
1 cup water
1 (13.5-ounce) can coconut milk

1. In the slow cooker, stir together the beef chuck, Yellow Curry Paste, potatoes, onions, fish sauce, and water.

2. Cook on low for 6 to 8 hours, or on high for 5 to 7 hours.

3. Add the coconut milk, and adjust the seasoning by adding more fish sauce as desired. Continue to cook for 10 minutes, until heated through.

4. Serve with jasmine rice.

Cooking tip: To offset the richness of the curry, serve with a Thai Cucumber Salad (page 105). The combination of dishes creates a winning contrast of crunchy, sweet, and spicy. This curry is mild, so if you enjoy spice, be sure to add the full amount of chiles in the salad for a meal with a little kick.

Beef Massaman Curry

kaeng masamun neua

SOY-FREE | NUT-FREE | QUICK PREP Perfumed with cardamom, cloves, star anise, and cumin, this curry fills your kitchen with a heavenly aroma while cooking. Come home to this mild yet classic curry, and be warmed by these flavorful spices and the richness of coconut milk. Pineapple adds even more sweetness, creating a stark contrast from other curries. Use either fresh pineapple or canned. If using canned, choose one in a low-sugar syrup, and be sure to drain the syrup well before adding the pineapple to the slow cooker.

SERVES 6
PREP TIME: 10 MINUTES
COOK TIME: 6 TO 8 HOURS ON LOW,
5 TO 7 HOURS ON HIGH

1 cup Massaman Curry Paste
   (page 130) or store bought
1½ pounds beef chuck, cut into
   2-inch pieces
1 pound Yukon Gold or red potatoes,
   cut into 2-inch chunks
2 onions, halved and sliced
1 cup water
2 tablespoons palm sugar
¼ cup fish sauce
¼ cup freshly squeezed lime juice
2 (13.5-ounce) cans coconut milk
1 cup diced pineapple

1. In the slow cooker, stir together the Massaman Curry Paste, beef chuck, potatoes, onions, water, palm sugar, fish sauce, and lime juice.

2. Cook on low for 6 to 8 hours, or on high for 5 to 7 hours.

3. Add the coconut milk and pineapple, and continue to cook for 10 minutes, until heated through. Adjust the flavors as desired, adding more fish sauce, palm sugar, or lime juice as needed.

4. Serve with jasmine rice.

Beef Red Curry

kaeng phed neua

SOY-FREE | NUT-FREE | QUICK PREP Red curry paste is a flavor ubiquitous in Thai cuisine, as it lends its mix of seasonings to countless dishes beyond curries, such as fish cakes and sausages. When it is used as a curry base, the result is a fiery hot, soupy dish loaded with character. Beef adds a buttery richness to this slow cooker favorite, and because it can withstand longer cooking times without losing texture or flavor, it's great for making on a long day away from home. Just add a smaller quantity of curry paste if using one commercially prepared, to avoid an unpleasantly spicy dish.

SERVES 6
PREP TIME: 10 MINUTES
COOK TIME: 6 TO 8 HOURS ON LOW,
5 TO 7 HOURS ON HIGH

1½ pounds beef top round,
  thinly sliced
1 cup water
¾ to 1 cup Red Curry Paste
  (page 128) or store bought
1 cup bamboo shoots
1 red bell pepper, cut into strips
1 onion, halved and sliced
¼ cup fish sauce
2 tablespoons palm sugar
3 serrano chiles
1 (13.5-ounce) can coconut milk
1 cup fresh Thai basil
Cilantro, for garnish

1. In the slow cooker, stir together the beef, water, Red Curry Paste, bamboo shoots, bell pepper, onion, fish sauce, and palm sugar.

2. Cook on low for 6 to 8 hours, or on high for 5 to 7 hours.

3. Cut lengthwise slits into the serrano chiles, and add the chiles and the coconut milk to the slow cooker. Cover and cook for 10 minutes.

4. Adjust the flavors as desired, adding more fish sauce or palm sugar.

5. Add the Thai basil and stir until wilted, about 1 minute.

6. Garnish with cilantro and serve with jasmine rice.

Cooking tip: Many different cuts of meat can be used to make a curry. However, when preparing the beef, be sure to cut it into small, bite-size pieces, as it cooks more evenly and makes a better presentation come mealtime.

Beef Penang Curry

kaeng penang neua

SOY-FREE | QUICK PREP Derived from Malaysian cooking, this dish combines Thai flavors in the paste while still including peanuts, a popular element in Malay cuisine. Note that in this recipe, sweet basil is used—a contrast from other curries that favor the stronger Thai basil.

SERVES 6
PREP TIME: 10 MINUTES
COOK TIME: 6 TO 8 HOURS ON LOW,
5 TO 7 HOURS ON HIGH

¾ cup Penang Curry Paste (page 131)
   or store bought
1 cup water
1½ pounds beef chuck, cut into
   2-inch chunks
2 large Thai chiles, sliced lengthwise
1 tablespoon palm sugar
2 tablespoons fish sauce
1 (13.5-ounce) can coconut milk
¼ cup dry roasted peanuts
½ cup loosely packed
   sweet basil leaves

1. In the slow cooker, stir together the Penang Curry Paste, water, beef chuck, Thai chiles, palm sugar, and fish sauce.

2. Cook on low for 6 to 8 hours, or on high for 5 to 7 hours.

3. Add the coconut milk and peanuts, and cook for an additional 10 minutes.

4. Adjust the flavors as desired, adding more fish sauce or palm sugar.

5. Add the sweet basil leaves and stir until wilted, about 1 minute.

6. Serve with jasmine rice.

Beef Jungle Curry ~ *kaeng pah neua*

SOY-FREE | QUICK PREP **If heat is what you are after, this is the curry for you.** This Northern curry uses no coconut milk to mask the heat but instead takes your mouth on a journey through the herbaceous jungles of Thailand. Jungle curry paste is notable for its spice, but also for its inclusion of a variety of herbs that makes it complex and delicious. Buy jungle curry paste premade, or for optimum flavor and spice level control, make it yourself (page 133).

SERVES 6
PREP TIME: 10 MINUTES
COOK TIME: 6 TO 8 HOURS ON LOW,
5 TO 7 HOURS ON HIGH

1 cup Jungle Curry Paste (page 133)
  or store bought
1½ pounds beef stew meat, cut into
  2-inch chunks
1 pound kabocha, peeled, cored,
  and cut into 1-inch pieces
1 cup bamboo shoots
1 cup yard-long beans, cut into
  1-inch segments
4 cups water
1 cup quartered Thai eggplant
¼ cup fish sauce
2 tablespoons palm sugar
½ cup loosely packed Thai basil leaves

1. In the slow cooker, stir together the Jungle Curry Paste, beef, kabocha, bamboo shoots, beans, and water.

2. Cook on low for 6 to 8 hours, or on high 5 to 7 hours.

3. Add the eggplant, fish sauce, and palm sugar, and continue to cook for 10 additional minutes. Taste and adjust the flavors if desired, adding additional fish sauce or palm sugar.

4. Add the Thai basil leaves, and stir until wilted, about 1 minute.

5. Serve with jasmine rice.

Cooking tip: Jungle curry is a thin, watery curry. If you prefer your curry a little thicker, add a few tablespoons of roasted rice powder (see the Thai Chicken Salad recipe on page 84) at the end of cooking to thicken it up a bit.

Spinach Pork Curry

gang tay po

SOY-FREE | NUT-FREE | QUICK PREP Similar to a red curry, this mouthwatering dish is laced to perfection with the sour notes of tamarind. Tender and succulent, pork belly is the star of the show in this preparation. This dish is traditionally made using water spinach, but because it is hard to find in the States, this recipe replaces it with spinach. If you can find a source for water spinach, called *pak bung*, morning glory vine, or swamp cabbage, substitute it here.

SERVES 4 TO 6
PREP TIME: 10 MINUTES
COOK TIME: 6 TO 8 HOURS ON LOW,
5 TO 7 HOURS ON HIGH

1½ pounds pork belly, skin removed
  and sliced
½ cup Red Curry Paste (page 128)
  or store bought
2 cups Pork Stock (page 120)
  or store bought, or water
2 tablespoons fish sauce
Juice of 1 key lime
2 tablespoons tamarind paste
1 tablespoon palm sugar
1 (13.5-ounce) can coconut milk
1 bunch spinach, chopped

Ingredient tip: Pork belly can be difficult to find at a standard grocery store, but it is readily available at any Asian market—and for the best price, as well.

1. In the slow cooker, stir together the pork belly, Red Curry Paste, and Pork Stock.

2. Cook on low for 6 to 8 hours, or on high for 5 to 7 hours.

3. Add the fish sauce, lime juice, tamarind paste, palm sugar, coconut milk, and spinach. Continue to cook for 10 minutes. Adjust the seasonings as desired, adding more tamarind, fish sauce, or palm sugar.

4. Serve with jasmine rice.

Sweet Pork ~ *mu wan*

SOY-FREE | NUT-FREE | QUICK PREP   Here's another simple, nourishing recipe perfectly adaptable to slow cooking. Using a pork tenderloin to create a tender, juicy topping for a bowl of jasmine rice has never been easier! Simply mix a few ingredients, come home hours later to a house that smells fantastic, and you have a super simple meal with no fuss. Serve with a spicy accompaniment, such as Papaya Salad (page 104) or Green Mango Salad (page 107).

SERVES 4 TO 6
PREP TIME: 5 MINUTES
COOK TIME: 4 TO 6 HOURS ON LOW

1 pound pork tenderloin

1 teaspoon freshly ground
   white pepper

1 cup Pork Stock (page 120)
   or store bought

8 garlic cloves, chopped

4 tablespoons vegetable oil

3 tablespoons fish sauce

5 tablespoons golden brown sugar

1. On a large plate, coat the pork tenderloin with the white pepper. Place it in the bottom of the slow cooker.

2. In a medium bowl, stir together the Pork Stock, garlic, oil, fish sauce, and brown sugar, dissolving the brown sugar. Pour the mixture into the slow cooker. Roll the pork loin in the sauce to coat, and cover the slow cooker.

3. Cook on low for 4 to 6 hours.

4. Slice the pork tenderloin into thin medallions, and serve with jasmine rice.

Pork Meatloaf 🌿 *mu yoa*

NUT-FREE | QUICK PREP Dishes like meatloaf may seem entirely Western at first glance. However, variations of the minced meatloaf exist in many cultures, including this one, which combines Thai flavors of garlic, white pepper, and soy sauce. Try it with rice for a simple meal, or add it to stir-fries or even to an omelet for a uniquely Thai twist on your cooking.

SERVES 6 TO 8
PREP TIME: 10 MINUTES
COOK TIME: 4 HOURS ON LOW

Nonstick cooking spray
2 pounds ground pork
20 garlic cloves, minced
3 tablespoons thick soy sauce
2 tablespoons white peppercorns

Ingredient tip: White peppercorns, like black ones, are most flavorful when freshly ground. However, if you can't find whole white peppercorns, use ground instead. Ground white pepper is much more readily available and can be substituted in equal proportion for whole peppercorns.

1. Line the slow cooker with aluminum foil by crossing two sheets perpendicular over one another, allowing the extra foil to hang over the slow cooker insert. The extra pieces will be used as handles to remove the meatloaf from the slow cooker. Spray the foil with the nonstick cooking spray.

2. In a large bowl, stir together the pork, garlic, and soy sauce.

3. In a mortar or spice grinder, coarsely grind the white peppercorns, and add them to the pork mixture. Using clean hands, mix the ingredients well.

4. Transfer the pork mixture to the slow cooker, pressing it down into an even layer.

5. Cook on low for 4 hours.

6. Remove, slice, and serve with rice or sautéed with vegetables.

Pork Rib Curry ✦ *gar doog mu hung le*

SOY-FREE | NUT-FREE **This simple, spicy curry features pork ribs, while notably omitting the coconut milk. It is a thin, watery curry that is light, yet filling and delicious. The white peppercorns give it a unique flavor that leaves you hankering for more. Serve it with a generous amount of rice to counter the heat.**

SERVES 4 TO 6

PREP TIME: 15 MINUTES

COOK TIME: 6 TO 8 HOURS ON LOW, 5 TO 7 HOURS ON HIGH

¼ cup Red Curry Paste (page 128) or store bought

5 Thai chiles

1 teaspoon shrimp paste

1 teaspoon white peppercorns

1½ teaspoons salt

6 cups water

2½ pounds pork spareribs, cut lengthwise across the bone into 2-inch-wide racks

1 tablespoon palm sugar

1. In a blender, food processor, or mortar, process the Red Curry Paste, chiles, shrimp paste, and white peppercorns until they form a moist paste. If using a blender or food processor, use a bit of water to aid the process. Transfer the paste to the slow cooker.

2. In the slow cooker, stir together the salt, water, and pork ribs.

3. Cook on low for 6 to 8 hours, or on high for 5 to 7 hours.

4. Add the palm sugar, stirring to dissolve.

5. Serve with jasmine rice.

Cooking tip: Red Curry Paste is inherently hot, so when additional chiles are added, the dish can become seriously scorching. If you like the heat, go for it—even add more, if you can handle it. But if you're not a fan of superhot foods, cut back on the quantity, or substitute a milder variety in place of the Thai chiles.

Pork Coconut Curry ❧

SOY-FREE | NUT-FREE | QUICK PREP **An example of a fantastic, nontraditional Thai curry,**
this pork coconut curry uses authentic Thai flavors, while requiring no premade
curry paste. Designed for quick prep so that you can have dinner in the pot and
cooking in minutes, this is a perfect weeknight meal that is incredibly fragrant and
requires few ingredients. Drawing on the flavors of yellow curry,
it is a mild curry suitable for all.

SERVES 4 TO 6
PREP TIME: 10 MINUTES
COOK TIME: 6 TO 8 HOURS ON LOW,
4 HOURS ON HIGH

2 pounds boneless pork chops,
    cut into 2-inch pieces
Salt and pepper
1 large onion, sliced
2 tablespoons minced ginger
4 garlic cloves, minced
1 tablespoon ground cumin
1 tablespoon curry powder
1 small tomato, diced
2 cups Chicken Stock (page 118)
    or store bought
1 (13.5-ounce) can coconut milk

1. Place the pork in the slow cooker and season well
with salt and pepper.

2. Add the onion, ginger, garlic, cumin, curry powder,
tomato, and Chicken Stock. Stir well, cover and cook
for 4 hours on high or 6 to 8 hours on low.

3. Add the coconut milk to the slow cooker, stir
to incorporate, cover, and continue to cook for
10 minutes to heat through. Serve over jasmine rice.

Ingredient tip: Whole spices maintain flavor much longer than
ground spices, which is of benefit for slow-cooked food where
spices can become muted over the long cooking time. For the
most flavor when making this dish or any other, grind cumin
seeds directly before using. A mortar and pestle or a cleaned
coffee grinder work best, but in a pinch a food processor can
manage the task as well.

9

SALADS AND SIDES

....

Papaya Salad ~ *som tum*

SOY-FREE **This classic dish is a must for anyone delving into preparing Thai food at home. A perfect combination of salty, sour, and sweet, papaya salad is simple to make right at home. Once you've finished, give it a taste, and if needed, adjust the seasonings, adding more lime juice, fish sauce, or palm sugar as desired.**

SERVES 4 TO 6
PREP TIME: 20 MINUTES

6 garlic cloves

3 Thai chiles

1 tablespoon palm sugar

2 tablespoons dried shrimp, soaked in warm water for 10 minutes

¾ cup yard-long beans, cut into 1-inch segments

8 cherry tomatoes, halved

4 cups shredded green papaya

¼ cup freshly squeezed lime juice

3 tablespoons fish sauce

¼ cup dry roasted peanuts

1. In a mortar, grind the garlic until broken into small pieces. Add the chiles, and pound until broken apart in many pieces.

2. In a small bowl, microwave the palm sugar for 20 seconds, until slightly softened, and add it to the mortar, pounding to incorporate. Add the shrimp and yard-long beans to the mortar, and pound to break up the shrimp and bruise the beans. Add the tomatoes, and lightly pound to release a bit of juice.

3. Add the papaya, and mix well.

4. Add the lime juice, fish sauce, and peanuts; mix again to incorporate; and serve.

Cooking tip: If you don't have a mortar large enough to accommodate this recipe, use a sturdy stainless-steel bowl with a pestle to achieve the same results. In this case, you are not grinding the ingredients to create a paste, just breaking them apart to release their juices and flavor the entire dish.

Thai Cucumber Salad

nam thaeng kwa

SOY-FREE | NUT-FREE | QUICK PREP A cooling food, the cucumber naturally pairs well with the spicy curries and meats of Thai cooking. While this salad calls for chiles, you can make it as hot or mild as you like by adjusting the quantity or type of chile used. For more spice, add Thai chiles. If you prefer less, choose a larger chile, such as a Fresno chile, for a considerably milder heat.

SERVES 4 TO 6
PREP TIME: 10 MINUTES

¾ cup distilled white vinegar

¾ cup brown sugar

½ teaspoon salt

2 large cucumbers, quartered
   lengthwise and thinly sliced

2 serrano chiles, chopped finely

¼ cup roughly chopped fresh cilantro

1. In a small saucepan, bring the vinegar, sugar, and salt to a boil for about 1 minute, stirring to dissolve the sugar and salt. Turn off the heat, and set aside to cool.

2. Add the cucumbers and chiles to a medium bowl.

3. Pour the cooled dressing over them, and toss to coat.

4. Add the cilantro, mix well, and serve.

Cooking tip: Make the dressing the day before to reduce prep time when you plan on eating this salad. Store it in an airtight container in the refrigerator, and toss with the remaining ingredients right before serving to maintain crispness.

Bean Salad with Crispy Shallots *yam tua poo*

SOY-FREE | NUT-FREE   A light bean salad, this mild dish pairs with curries of all sorts or can be eaten as a meal on its own along with rice. For the best flavor, enjoy this salad at the height of summer, when fresh green beans are at their peak.

SERVES 4 TO 6
PREP TIME: 15 MINUTES

1½ pounds green beans,
   halved diagonally
1½ tablespoons Chile-Tamarind Paste
   (page 125) or store bought
½ cup freshly squeezed lemon juice
2 tablespoons fish sauce
2 tablespoons palm sugar
2 Thai chiles, finely sliced
6 tablespoons Crispy Shallots
   (page 126)

1. Bring a large pot of water to a boil. Submerge the beans in the water, and blanch for 1 minute. Remove the beans to a colander, and run them under cold water to quickly stop the cooking process.

2. In a blender, process the Chile-Tamarind Paste, lemon juice, fish sauce, and palm sugar until well combined.

3. In a large bowl, toss the beans with the chiles. Pour the dressing over the beans, and toss to combine.

4. Arrange on a large platter, and serve topped with the Crispy Shallots.

Green Mango Salad

yam mamuang kap het nang fa

SOY-FREE Similar to papaya salad, this sweet, sour, and spicy salad is made with unripe mango. Meanwhile, fresh mint and cilantro combine to give the dish an herbal quality with biting heat. Find unripe mangos at an Asian market to prepare this crunchy salad; then pair it with sticky rice, a mild curry, or roasted hens.

SERVES 4 TO 6
PREP TIME: 15 MINUTES

3 green mangos
1 garlic clove
2 Thai chiles
2 shallots, sliced
1 tablespoon palm sugar
3 tablespoons fish sauce
⅓ cup freshly squeezed lime juice
¼ cup chopped fresh cilantro
¼ cup dry roasted peanuts
¼ cup chopped mint leaves

1. Remove the skin from the mangos, and shred their flesh using a grater, hand grating tool, or food processor. Place the shredded mango in a large bowl.

2. In a mortar, crush the garlic until broken apart. Add the chiles to the mortar, pounding them until broken into several pieces. Add the shallots, and pound them several times.

3. In a small bowl, microwave the palm sugar for 20 seconds, until slightly softened, and add it to the mortar, pounding to incorporate. Add the fish sauce and lime juice.

4. Transfer this mixture to the bowl with the mango, and stir to combine.

5. Add the cilantro, peanuts, and mint, and serve.

Cooking tip: The seeds and membranes of chiles are the hottest part. To slightly moderate the heat, when you stem the chiles, knock out the seeds. If you like the extra heat, on the other hand, feel free to leave them in.

Pomelo Salad ~ *yam som-o*

SOY-FREE   For many Westerners, pomelo is a strange fruit. However, in Asian cuisine, the pomelo is viewed as winter's prized treat. Similar in flavor to other citrus, the pomelo tastes like a grapefruit, but without its characteristic tartness. Serve this zesty salad on a cold winter day, and receive a welcome burst of spice and vitamin C.

SERVES 4 TO 6
PREP TIME: 15 MINUTES

3 large pomelos, peeled
2 tablespoons palm sugar
1 small shallot, thinly sliced
3 tablespoons fish sauce
2 Thai chiles, finely sliced
2 garlic cloves
¼ cup crushed cashews,
   lightly toasted
¼ cup mint leaves

1. Using a sharp knife, cut the segments of the pomelos away from the membranes and set aside.

2. In a medium bowl, soften the palm sugar by microwaving it for 10 to 20 seconds. Mix in the shallot, fish sauce, chiles, and garlic. Squeeze the membranes of the pomelo over the bowl to express any remaining juices.

3. Stir in the pomelo, cashews, and mint. Mix well and serve immediately or refrigerate.

Cooking tip: Pomelo has very fibrous membranes that need to be removed from the flesh before serving. When carefully trimmed, most of the white membrane can be successfully eliminated, but you may need to trim the segments further. Any white, pithy areas should be cut off, as these can be quite tough.

Jicama and Pomelo Salad *yam man kaeo*

SOY-FREE   Another take on the pomelo salad pairs the flavorful citrus fruit with jicama, a root vegetable hailing from Central America. While its outward appearance bears resemblance to a beige turnip, peeling its skin reveals a crisp, sweet flesh that can work seamlessly with fruit and vegetable salads alike.

SERVES 6
PREP TIME: 15 MINUTES

1 pomelo, peeled
2 tablespoons palm sugar
2 garlic cloves, chopped
2 Thai chiles, thinly sliced
1 tablespoon fish sauce
1 jicama, peeled and cut
   into matchsticks
1 cup bean sprouts
1 cup thinly sliced napa cabbage
2 tablespoons crushed,
   roasted peanuts
3 tablespoons Crispy Shallots
   (page 126)

Ingredient tip: When shopping for jicama, look for unblemished roots that are firm and heavy. Select a smaller root, under 3 pounds, as these tend to be the juiciest. Jicama doesn't need to be refrigerated, but a cool location around 60°F is ideal, so a root cellar or basement is the optimal storage location.

1. Using a sharp knife, cut the segments of the pomelo away from the membranes.

2. In a small bowl, microwave the palm sugar for 10 to 20 seconds to soften.

3. In a large bowl, mix together the palm sugar, garlic, chiles, and fish sauce.

4. Stir in the pomelo, jicama, bean sprouts, and cabbage. Mix in the peanuts.

5. Top the salad with the Crispy Shallots and serve.

Stir-Fried Chinese Broccoli Greens

phat khanaeng

NUT-FREE | QUICK PREP **This is a simple, classic, easy to reproduce Thai side dish. Use Chinese broccoli, a member of the cabbage family often labeled as *gai laan* or *kai laan* at Asian grocers. With edible flowers, tender stems, and leafy greens, Chinese broccoli is a terrific option for sautéing. If you have difficulty sourcing it, substitute its hybrid, patented cousin, broccolini.**

SERVES 4 TO 6
PREP TIME: 5 MINUTES
COOK TIME: 10 MINUTES

2 tablespoons vegetable oil

8 garlic cloves, halved and smashed

6 cups Chinese broccoli, diced into
   1-inch pieces

1 tablespoon fish sauce

1 tablespoon thin soy sauce

3 tablespoons yellow bean sauce

½ cup water

1 teaspoon sugar

⅛ teaspoon freshly ground
   white pepper

1. In a large wok or skillet, heat the oil. Add the garlic and sauté until fragrant, just a few seconds. Immediately add the greens, stirring constantly until lightly wilted, about 2 minutes.

2. Add the fish sauce, soy sauce, yellow bean sauce, water, sugar, and white pepper.

3. Continue stirring until the broccoli stems are cooked through and tender, 3 to 4 more minutes, and serve.

Cooking tip: If you don't have yellow bean sauce on hand, substitute oyster sauce here for a similar flavor.

Spring Rolls ~ *popla thot*

SOY-FREE | NUT-FREE **Spring rolls make a welcome savory accompaniment to just about any meal. Thai spring rolls are most often a vegetarian variety, and here a combination of carrots, mushrooms, tofu, egg, and rice noodles form the filling. Pair these with the Sweet-Spicy Chile Dipping Sauce (page 122), and enjoy this easy appetizer over a glass of wine or cold beer before the main course.**

MAKES 10 ROLLS
PREP TIME: 20 MINUTES
COOK TIME: 15 MINUTES

4 garlic cloves, crushed

2 tablespoons vegetable oil, plus more for frying

½ cup finely diced carrots

5 dried black mushrooms, soaked for 15 minutes and finely diced

¼ cup finely diced cabbage

¼ cup bean sprouts

¾ cup finely diced tofu

1 egg

½ cup glass noodles, soaked for 15 minutes

1 tablespoon thin soy sauce

1 teaspoon sugar

½ teaspoon salt

½ teaspoon freshly ground white pepper

10 spring roll wrappers

1. In a wok or skillet, fry the garlic in the oil over medium heat just until it becomes fragrant.

2. Add the carrot and stir to combine. Add the mushrooms, cabbage, bean sprouts, tofu, egg, and noodles, stirring a few times between each addition. Add the soy sauce, sugar, salt, and white pepper. Transfer the mixture to another dish to cool.

3. Prepare a small bowl of water for sealing the spring roll wrappers. Line up 3 or 4 spring roll wrappers on a clean surface. Add about 1 tablespoon of filling to each wrapper. Working one at a time, fold the sides inward, and roll it away from you so that it is tightly wrapped. Use your finger or a small brush to apply water to the open edge, and press to seal. Repeat until all the spring rolls are filled.

4. Add 2 to 3 inches of oil to the bottom of a large pot. Over high heat, bring the oil temperature to 350°F.

5. Deep-fry the spring rolls in the hot oil for 3 to 5 minutes, or until uniformly crisp and browned. Remove the spring rolls from the oil to a plate lined with paper towels to drain.

6. Serve with the Sweet-Spicy Chile Dipping Sauce (page 122).

Chicken Satay with Peanut Dipping Sauce

satay kai

SOY-FREE One of the most well-known street foods, Thai chicken satay is spicy, marinated chicken with just enough heat to wake up your taste buds. Marinating the chicken breasts overnight provides the most robust flavor, but aim for at least 3 to 4 hours in the refrigerator before cooking. Grilling is the traditional preparation method, but broiling in your oven allows you to create this succulent dish any time of the year.

SERVES 4
PREP TIME: 15 MINUTES, PLUS 3 TO
24 HOURS TO MARINATE
COOK TIME: 10 TO 15 MINUTES

FOR THE SATAY

1 cup coconut milk

3 tablespoons Penang Curry Paste
   (page 131) or store bought

2 tablespoons brown sugar

2 tablespoons fish sauce

1 teaspoon ground coriander

1 pound boneless, skinless
   chicken breasts

FOR THE PEANUT SAUCE

¾ cup coconut milk

3 tablespoons Massaman Curry Paste
   (page 130)

⅓ cup peanut butter

3 tablespoons brown sugar

2 tablespoons fish sauce

TO MAKE THE SATAY

1. In a medium bowl, stir together the coconut milk, Penang Curry Paste, brown sugar, fish sauce, and coriander.

2. Cut each chicken breast in half horizontally, and then slice each piece into strips 1 inch wide by 3 inches long. Combine the chicken with the marinade, cover, and refrigerate for 3 to 24 hours.

TO MAKE THE PEANUT SAUCE

In a small saucepan over medium heat, heat the coconut milk until it begins steaming. Add the Massaman Curry Paste, stirring to combine, and cook for 2 minutes. Add the peanut butter, and stir until incorporated. Add the brown sugar and fish sauce, stir, and turn off the heat. Cool and refrigerate for up to 1 week before using.

TO MAKE THE SKEWERS

1. If you are using bamboo skewers, soak them for at least 30 minutes prior to threading the meat to prevent scorching. Push 2 to 3 pieces of chicken on to each skewer.

2. Preheat the broiler.

3. Broil the skewers for 4 minutes before flipping them. Cook the other side for 4 to 5 minutes. If necessary, flip again until they are cooked through.

4. Serve the satay on a serving platter with the dipping sauce.

Cooking tip: If you prefer, these can be made on a charcoal or gas grill. Simply prepare the grill by starting a fire, or preheating if you have a gas grill. Start by grilling for 4 minutes on each side, flipping as needed to prevent burning. Check for doneness after cooking on each side, flipping again if necessary.

Curry Puffs ~ *karipap*

SOY-FREE | NUT-FREE | QUICK PREP These tantalizing snacks are a street food mainstay in Thailand and Malaysia. Filled with a succulent potato chicken curry and wrapped with a buttery, flaky dough, they are equally perfect for snacking on the go or serving as an appetizer or party food. Mild in spice, they are universally appealing. Make the filling in your slow cooker, and you are halfway there. Create a stiff dough, and fill away.

SERVES 6
PREP TIME: 10 MINUTES, PLUS
30 MINUTES TO REST
COOK TIME: 6½ HOURS ON LOW

FOR THE FILLING

1 cup finely diced chicken breast

1 cup diced onion

1 cup diced potato, skinned

1½ tablespoons curry powder

1½ teaspoons salt

½ teaspoon freshly ground
   white pepper

3 tablespoons sugar

3 tablespoons butter

½ cup water

FOR THE DOUGH

3⅓ cups all-purpose flour

½ teaspoon salt

10 tablespoons butter

¾ cup water

Vegetable oil, for deep-frying

TO MAKE THE FILLING

1. In the slow cooker, stir together the chicken, onion, potato, curry powder, salt, white pepper, sugar, butter, and water.

2. Cook on low for 6 hours. Remove the lid and continue to cook the filling for an additional 30 minutes, or until much of the water evaporates and the filling is slightly dry. Cool the filling.

TO MAKE THE DOUGH

1. In a large bowl, mix the flour and salt. Cut the butter into small pieces, and using a pastry knife, incorporate it into the flour until the mixture resembles sand. Add the water and knead the dough until it is firm and all the flour is incorporated. Cover the bowl with a clean kitchen towel, and let the dough rest for 30 minutes.

2. Roll the dough into a log about 2 inches in diameter. Cut off ½-inch wide chunks and roll each into a thin round about 3 inches in diameter. As you work, fill the rounds with 2 heaping teaspoons of the cooled filling, and bring the sides together to form a half moon. Crimp the edges together to seal. Arrange the curry puffs on a tray as you work.

3. In a large pot or wok, add 3 inches of vegetable oil, and bring the oil to 350°F.

4. Working in batches, lower several curry puffs into the oil, taking care not to crowd the pan. Fry them for 3 to 5 minutes until the dough develops a golden color and becomes crisp. Remove the puffs from the oil, and drain on a few layers of paper towel.

5. Repeat with the remaining curry puffs and serve.

Cooking tip: These are a very customizable treat. If you prefer more heat, add a pinch or two of ground Thai chiles and a teaspoon of paprika to give the filling a red hue. If you enjoy cilantro and garlic, add them to the filling as well, along with any other favorite spices, to make your curry puffs just how you like them.

10

SAUCES AND PANTRY STAPLES

....

Chicken Stock

SOY-FREE | NUT-FREE | QUICK PREP Cilantro and garlic are the main flavor components in a Thai-flavored stock that differentiate it from a Western one. To make this light, flavorful stock, you can use discarded parts of the chicken, such as backs, necks, wing tips, and bones. Then really take the flavor up a notch, using this stock as a base for curries, soups, and stir-fries. Make a large batch while you are out for the day, and come home to a house that smells divine.

MAKES 3 QUARTS
PREP TIME: 5 MINUTES
COOK TIME: 6 TO 8 HOURS ON LOW

2 pounds chicken pieces (backs, necks, feet, bones, wing tips)

3 carrots, halved

1 onion, halved

2 to 3 inches daikon

1 bunch cilantro stems (reserve the leaves for a different recipe)

10 unpeeled garlic cloves, crushed

1 stalk lemongrass, roughly chopped

1 teaspoon black peppercorns

1. In the slow cooker, cover the chicken pieces, carrots, onion, daikon, cilantro stems, garlic, lemongrass, and peppercorns with cool water.

2. Cover and cook on low for 6 to 8 hours.

3. Pour the stock into a large bowl covered with a wire-mesh strainer, gently pressing the vegetables to extract liquid. Cool.

4. Pour the stock into lidded jars and refrigerate. Remove the layer of fat that accumulates on the top of the jar before using.

5. Refrigerate for 5 days, or freeze for up to 3 months.

Cooking tip: Make the stock overnight in your slow cooker to have it ready to use in the morning. If you plan to use the stock with a quick turnaround, and not refrigerate it in between, allow it to sit undisturbed for about 10 minutes; then, using a large spoon, scoop out the visible layer of oil that forms on its surface.

Vegetable Stock

SOY-FREE | NUT-FREE | QUICK PREP **Vegetarians need not avoid Thai soups—instead make vegetable stock to substitute in recipes calling for pork or chicken-based ones. This light yet flavorful vegetable-based stock can be used in equal exchange for any recipe calling for a meat-based stock. You'll find it creates soups of equivalent complexity to any made with meat.**

MAKES 3 QUARTS
PREP TIME: 10 MINUTES
COOK TIME: 6 TO 8 HOURS ON LOW

3 cups roughly chopped carrots

1½ cups roughly chopped onions

1 bunch cilantro stems (reserve the leaves for another recipe)

10 unpeeled garlic cloves, crushed

1 teaspoon black peppercorns

2 stalks lemongrass, cut into chunks

1. In the slow cooker, cover the carrots, onions, cilantro stems, garlic, peppercorns, and lemongrass with cool water.

2. Cover and cook on low for 6 to 8 hours.

3. Pour the stock into a large bowl covered with a wire-mesh strainer, gently pressing the vegetables to extract liquid.

4. Use immediately, or cool to room temperature and refrigerate for up to 5 days, or freeze for up to 3 months.

Cooking tip: When cilantro stems are removed from the leaves, the shelf life of the leaves deteriorates quickly. So when using cilantro stems in making stock, plan on using the leaves within a day or two. Conversely, if you use the leaves for another recipe, you can freeze the stems until you are ready to make a stock, and add them to the slow cooker without defrosting.

Pork Stock

SOY-FREE | NUT-FREE | QUICK PREP Pork Stock creates a richly flavored soup like no other. Common in stir-fries and soups, it delivers a subtle flavor that is quite distinctive. Store the stock in the refrigerator, or portion it into an ice cube tray or muffin tin, and freeze individual portions for use in a variety of dishes.

MAKES 3 QUARTS
PREP TIME: 10 MINUTES
COOK TIME: 6 TO 8 HOURS ON LOW

3 pounds pork bones

1 stalk lemongrass, roughly chopped

5 to 6 inches daikon, sliced

10 unpeeled garlic cloves, crushed

½ bunch cilantro stems (reserve the leaves for another recipe)

1 teaspoon black peppercorns

1. In the slow cooker, cover the pork bones, lemongrass, daikon, garlic, cilantro stems, and peppercorns with cool water.

2. Cover and cook on low for 6 to 8 hours.

3. Pour the stock into a large bowl covered with a wire-mesh strainer, gently pressing the vegetables to extract liquid.

4. Use immediately, or cover and refrigerate for up to 5 days, or freeze for up to 3 months.

Cooking tip: Find pork bones for making soup in a well-stocked supermarket or Asian market, or directly from a butcher. If you have access and storage space, buying a whole or half pig will net you an abundance of bones for soup making, as well as provide high-quality meat not readily available in most grocery stores.

Chile Dipping Sauce

nam phrik

SOY-FREE | NUT-FREE | QUICK PREP **This is the standard Thai dipping sauce found just about anywhere Thai food is served. Using only four ingredients—lime juice, fish sauce, chiles, and garlic—this is the perfect sauce to spoon over soups, curries, rice, seafood, or fish to liven up the flavor. The sauce can be easily whipped up on demand, and refrigerated for up to 2 weeks in a tightly closed container.**

MAKES ⅓ CUP
PREP TIME: 5 MINUTES

6 tablespoons freshly squeezed
   lime juice
2 tablespoons fish sauce
6 Thai chiles, thinly sliced
1 garlic clove, minced

Ingredient tip: If you don't have access to Thai chiles, no problem. You can substitute 3 serrano chiles in this recipe to create a similarly spicy dish. Avoid using dried peppers in the sauce, though, as fresh peppers give a far superior bite to this excellent sauce.

In a small bowl, stir together the lime juice, fish sauce, chiles, and garlic. Serve.

Sweet-Spicy Chile Dipping Sauce

nam jeem kai yang

SOY-FREE | NUT-FREE | QUICK PREP   One of the best things about Thai food is the blend of sweet and spicy. While this dipping sauce has considerable heat, its sweetness makes it palatable to people who don't favor overly spicy foods. Make the sauce in advance to give it time to cool before serving—you can store it in the refrigerator for up to 5 days. Serve it alongside main dishes like Slow Cooker "Roasted" Hens (page 87) as well as appetizers like Spring Rolls (page 111).

SERVES 6
COOK TIME: 10 MINUTES

1 cup water

1 cup granulated sugar

¼ cup rice vinegar

1 teaspoon salt

½ teaspoon dried chili powder

1 teaspoon chopped cilantro leaves

1. In a small pot, mix together the water, sugar, vinegar, salt, and chili powder, and bring to a boil over medium-high heat. Turn the burner down to low, and simmer the sauce for 10 minutes.

2. Turn off the heat, and cool to room temperature.

3. Garnish with the cilantro and serve.

Chile-Vinegar Dipping Sauce

phrik namsom

SOY-FREE | NUT-FREE | QUICK PREP Another classic Thai dipping sauce, *phrik namsom* is a super spicy topping most often employed as an addition to noodle dishes such as Pad Thai (page 55) or noodle soups. Spoon some over a bowl of Beef Noodle Soup (page 52) or Tofu Glass Noodle Soup (page 53) to turn the heat up a notch. In Thailand, the chiles are eaten, but if you prefer, using just the sauce is fine too, as it will have plenty of heat especially after a more extended maceration period.

MAKES ¼ CUP
PREP TIME: 5 MINUTES

¼ cup distilled white vinegar
6 red Thai chiles, thinly sliced
½ teaspoon salt

Ingredient tip: If you prefer the flavor of fish sauce, exchange it here and omit the salt, using 1 teaspoon of a Thai fish sauce in its place. Serrano chiles can also be substituted, but cut back to about 2 chiles for a similar heat.

In a small bowl, stir together the vinegar, chiles, and salt. Let stand at room temperature for 20 minutes to allow flavors to mix. Store at room temperature for up to 4 days covered, or refrigerate for up to 2 weeks.

Tamarind Water ~ *nam som makham*

SOY-FREE | NUT-FREE| QUICK PREP **Tamarind is a widely used flavor component of countless Thai dishes. Providing a naturally sweet and sour flavor, it lends its distinct taste to sauces, soups, and curries. Tamarind is typically sold in blocks of pulp, necessitating the addition of water, a step called for in several recipes in this book.**

MAKES 1 CUP
PREP TIME: 5 MINUTES,
PLUS 20 MINUTES TO SOAK
COOK TIME: 10 MINUTES

1 cup hot water

2 ounces tamarind pulp
(about ¼ cup)

Ingredient tip: Tamarind is an astringent flavoring used in the same way lemon juice is used in the West. Similar in flavor to sour apricots and dates, the tamarind is a brown fruit contained in a leguminous pod. While the pods are widely available in some grocery stores, as well as in Asian and Indian markets, it is much quicker to process when you purchase a large block of the pulp, as called for in this recipe.

1. Heat the water in a kettle. Place the pulp in a heat-safe measuring cup or bowl. Pour the hot water over the pulp, and let it soak for 20 minutes.

2. Using clean hands, break apart the pulp gently.

3. Pour the pulp through a wire-mesh strainer with a bowl set underneath to catch the water. Press gently on the pulp to extract as much juice and pulp as possible.

4. For the best flavor, transfer the Tamarind Water to an airtight jar, and store it refrigerated for no more than 1 week.

Chile-Tamarind Paste *nam phrik pao*

SOY-FREE **The flavor of tom yam is derived from this spicy-sour condiment. Store-bought versions are readily available, but making this paste yourself is a fun and relatively easy process. Using the deep-frying process to bring out its rich flavor, this is the true distinctive taste of Thai cuisine.**

MAKES 1 CUP
PREP TIME: 15 MINUTES
COOK TIME: 10 MINUTES

1½ cups peanut oil
¾ cup shallots
¼ cup sliced garlic cloves
½ cup dried shrimp
10 large dried Thai chiles
2 tablespoons palm sugar
2 tablespoons fish sauce
3 tablespoons Tamarind Water
   (page 124) or concentrate

1. In a large wok or skillet, heat the oil. Add the shallots and garlic, and fry until golden brown. Promptly remove from the pan and drain.

2. Add the shrimp and chiles to the oil, and fry until they become golden brown. Remove and drain.

3. Add the garlic, shallots, shrimp, chiles, and palm sugar to a mortar, and grind until a uniform texture is achieved.

4. Add the fish sauce, Tamarind Water, and cooled oil from the wok. Continue to pound until the texture is fine.

5. Transfer the paste to an airtight container, and store refrigerated for up to 3 months.

Cooking tip: To save time, make this condiment in the food processor.

Crispy Shallots ✦

SOY-FREE | NUT-FREE The simple process of frying shallots creates a memorable flavor that graces many Thai stir-fried dishes and salads. Be sure to save the oil from frying for future use, as it lends great flavor to other dishes. Keep in mind that because you are frying, the hot oil will continue to cook the shallots even after removing them from the oil, so prompt removal from the pan once they become crisp is important.

MAKES 6 TABLESPOONS
PREP TIME: 5 MINUTES
COOK TIME: 20 MINUTES

6 shallots
1 cup vegetable oil

1. Cut the shallots in half and remove the peels. Thinly slice the shallots into strips.

2. In a large wok or skillet over high heat, heat the oil. When one shallot piece immediately bubbles on hitting the pan, add the remaining shallots and turn the heat to low, stirring occasionally and adjusting the heat as needed, so that the oil continues to fry the shallots.

3. Cook the shallots for 15 to 20 minutes, or until they are uniformly crisp and browned.

4. Pour the shallots and oil through a strainer set over a bowl. Allow the shallots to drain for several minutes; then transfer them to a paper towel until cool. Store the shallots in an airtight container at room temperature for 2 days.

5. Store the flavored oil in a separate airtight container for up to 2 weeks.

Cooking tip: If you want to skip frying the shallots yourself, fried shallots can be found at any Asian grocery store. However, when buying the shallots at the store, you miss out on the flavorful cooking oil, which is especially nice when cooking mildly flavored foods such as eggs and noodles.

Crispy Garlic

SOY-FREE | NUT-FREE | QUICK PREP Another classic meal topper, fried garlic provides the same garlic nuances to dishes without the intense bite of fresh garlic. While the recipe states vegetable oil as the frying medium, don't be wary of trying other oils as well. Palm oil and pork lard are both flavorful options for frying garlic, and if you have them on hand, they are great choices.

MAKES 6 TABLESPOONS
PREP TIME: 10 MINUTES
COOK TIME: 5 MINUTES

25 garlic cloves
1 cup vegetable oil

1. Peel and slice the garlic into thin pieces. For greatest uniformity, use a mandolin.

2. In a large wok or skillet, heat the oil over high heat. To test the oil, add a piece of garlic. If it begins frying immediately, the oil is ready. Add the remaining garlic to the pan, and turn the heat down to low.

3. Cook the garlic for 5 minutes, or until it becomes brown and crisp.

4. Pour the oil through a strainer set over a bowl to separate the garlic from the oil.

5. Transfer the garlic to a paper towel to drain and cool. Once the garlic is cool, refrigerate it in an airtight container for 2 days.

6. Refrigerate the garlic oil in an airtight container for up to 2 weeks.

Cooking tip: If the task of peeling garlic sounds like too much work to make this accompaniment, consider buying garlic already peeled. Sold in the refrigerated produce section, peeled garlic saves time, allowing you to create this flavorful condiment more quickly. Fried garlic is also available from Asian food stores.

Red Curry Paste

nam prik kaeng ped

SOY-FREE | NUT-FREE This is the most commonly used curry paste in Thai cooking, finding its way into curry dishes, soups, dips, sauces, and marinades. Considered one of the hottest of all the curry pastes, it pairs with chicken, beef, pork, and seafood. It is from this red curry paste that all other types of curry paste are derived, adding or exchanging ingredients to give the new pastes their own characteristics. This recipe makes enough for about 2 large batches of curry. Feel free to double, triple, or quadruple the recipe to cut down on kitchen work, but be sure to place the leftovers in the freezer. Unlike commercial brands, this paste contains no preservatives, making its refrigerated shelf life considerably shorter.

MAKES 1½ CUPS
PREP TIME: 30 MINUTES

5 dried New Mexico chiles, stemmed and seeded
5 dried Thai red chiles, stemmed and seeded
1 tablespoon coriander seeds
1 teaspoon cumin seeds
½ teaspoon black peppercorns
¾ cup chopped shallots
½ cup peeled garlic cloves
½ tablespoon finely chopped lime peel
2 lemongrass stalks, bottom inch removed, remaining lower stem sliced
⅓ cup chopped galangal
1 tablespoon shrimp paste

1. In a small bowl, cover the New Mexico and Thai chiles with water. Allow the chiles to soak for 30 minutes.

2. In a dry, hot skillet, toast the coriander, cumin seeds, and peppercorns until they sizzle and pop. Remove them from the heat, and transfer them to a bowl to cool.

3. Once cool, grind the coriander, cumin, and peppercorns with a mortar and pestle or a spice grinder, and transfer them to the bowl of a food processor.

4. Drain the chiles, reserving the soaking liquid. Add the chiles, shallots, garlic, lime peel, lemongrass, galangal, and shrimp paste to the food processor bowl, and process until finely ground. Add up to ½ cup of the soaking liquid from the chiles to enable the mixture to become a nice, moist paste.

5. Refrigerate in an airtight container for up to 1 month, or freeze for up to 3 months.

Cooking tip: When making curry pastes at home, you are able to control the heat. Using New Mexico chiles and just a few Thai chiles, this paste is not as hot as many red curry pastes commonly available. For a more intense heat, substitute some of the New Mexico chiles for more red Thai chiles.

Green Curry Paste *nam prik kaeng kiew wan*

SOY-FREE | NUT-FREE The delicate green color of this paste can be deceptive. Loaded with green chiles that give it its characteristic green hue, the herbal chile paste is quite hot. While the recipe calls for serrano chiles, you can increase the heat further by adding fresh green Thai chiles instead. This recipe produces enough paste to make a little more than two batches of green curry.

MAKES 2 CUPS
PREP TIME: 20 MINUTES

1½ teaspoons coriander seeds

1½ teaspoons cumin seeds

1 teaspoon white peppercorns

1 tablespoon finely chopped lime peel

¼ cup minced cilantro stems (reserve leaves for another recipe)

2 stalks lemongrass, bottom inch removed, remaining lower stem thinly sliced

⅓ cup minced galangal

1 inch turmeric root, minced

¼ cup chopped garlic

¾ cup chopped shallots

½ cup sliced serrano chiles

1 tablespoon shrimp paste

2 teaspoons salt

10 large leaves sweet basil

1. In a dry, hot skillet, toast the coriander seeds, cumin seeds, and white peppercorns until they begin to sizzle and become fragrant. Remove from the heat, and transfer to a bowl to cool.

2. Once cool, in a spice grinder or mortar, process the spices until they are powdered. Transfer them to the bowl of a food processor.

3. Add the lime peel, cilantro stems, lemongrass, galangal, turmeric, garlic, shallots, chiles, shrimp paste, salt, and basil to the food processor, and process until they form a paste.

4. Use the paste immediately, refrigerate in an airtight container for 1 month, or freeze for up to 3 months.

Cooking tip: Basil is used in this recipe to lend an herbal, colorful accent to the curry paste. If you don't have any basil on hand, several washed and dried lettuce leaves can be used in its place to give the paste a nice green color.

Massaman Curry Paste

nam prik kaeng masamun

SOY-FREE | NUT-FREE This Indian-influenced curry paste was brought to Thailand by the Muslim people who live in the southern region of the country. Popularized by its inclusion in the peanut satay sauce for dipping grilled meats, this perfumed curry paste is also used in stew-like curries. Using a mix of fresh and dry ingredients, this mild curry paste will make a flavorful addition to your kitchen.

MAKES 1 CUP
PREP TIME: 30 MINUTES

3 to 5 dried large red
   California chiles, stemmed
3 cardamom pods
¼ teaspoon black peppercorns
1 teaspoon cumin seeds
1 tablespoon coriander seeds
3 whole cloves
¼ teaspoon ground cinnamon
1 stalk lemongrass, bottom inch
   removed, remaining lower stem
   thinly sliced
1 tablespoon finely chopped galangal
¼ cup chopped garlic
⅓ cup chopped shallots
1 teaspoon shrimp paste

1. In a small bowl, cover the chiles with water. Soak for 30 minutes.

2. Remove the seeds from the cardamom pods. Place the cardamom seeds, peppercorns, cumin seeds, and coriander seeds in a hot, dry skillet, and toast over medium heat until fragrant. Shake the pan as the seeds are toasting to prevent burning.

3. Remove the seeds and place them in a bowl to cool. Transfer the mixture to the bowl of a food processor.

4. Drain the chiles, reserving the soaking liquid. Add the chiles, cloves, cinnamon, lemongrass, galangal, garlic, shallots, and shrimp paste to the food processor. Process until the mixture is finely ground. Add up to ½ cup of the soaking liquid to create a moist paste.

5. Use the paste immediately, or transfer it to an airtight container and refrigerate for up to 1 month, or freeze for up to 3 months.

Cooking tip: This curry paste is meant to be substantially milder than other pastes. However, if you prefer more heat than that produced by California chiles, substitute New Mexico chiles for a slightly spicier result.

Penang Curry Paste

nam prik kaeng phanaeng

SOY-FREE | NUT-FREE The name of this curry paste comes from the island of Penang, off the west coast of Malaysia. While its origins may not be Thai, this is one of many classic Thai curries combining a wide balance of flavors to create a variety of distinctive curry dishes.

MAKES 1½ CUPS
PREP TIME: 30 MINUTES

4 large New Mexico dried chiles, stemmed and seeded

1 red Thai chile, stemmed and seeded

1 tablespoon coriander seeds

1 teaspoon white peppercorns

1 finely chopped key lime rind

2 tablespoons shrimp paste

3 tablespoons chopped cilantro stems (reserve the leaves for another recipe)

2 tablespoons chopped galangal

⅓ cup chopped garlic

⅓ cup chopped shallots

1. In a small bowl, cover the New Mexico and Thai chiles with water. Soak for 30 minutes.

2. In a small pan over medium-high heat, dry roast the coriander seeds until fragrant, shaking to prevent burning. Remove them from the pan and set aside to cool.

3. In a mortar, grind the white peppercorns and cooled coriander seeds to a powder, and transfer them to the bowl of a food processor with the lime rind.

4. Drain the chiles, reserving the soaking liquid. Add the chiles, shrimp paste, cilantro stems, galangal, garlic, and shallots to the bowl of the food processor. Process until the mixture is a fine paste. Add up to ½ cup of the soaking liquid to aid in creating a moist paste.

5. Transfer the paste to an airtight container and refrigerate for up 1 month, or freeze it for up to 3 months.

Yellow Curry Paste ⬎ *krung kaeng kari*

SOY-FREE | NUT-FREE This mellow, sweet curry paste draws on the spices of Indian curry, while giving it a Thai infusion with mainstays such as lemongrass, shrimp paste, shallots, and chiles. This curry paste is most often used in flavoring a robust chicken curry with potatoes and onions.

MAKES 1 CUP
PREP TIME: 30 MINUTES

3 to 5 red dried California chiles, stemmed and seeded

1 tablespoon coriander seeds

1 tablespoon cumin seeds

3 tablespoons curry powder

2 tablespoons ground turmeric

1 tablespoon shrimp paste

2 stalks lemongrass, bottom inch removed and remaining lower stem thinly sliced

2 tablespoons minced ginger

3 tablespoons minced garlic

⅓ cup finely chopped shallots

1. In a small bowl, cover the chiles with water. Soak for 30 minutes.

2. In a small skillet over medium-high heat, roast the coriander and cumin seeds until fragrant, shaking the pan to prevent burning. Transfer the seeds to a bowl to cool.

3. Once cool, transfer the coriander and cumin, as well as the curry powder and turmeric, to a mortar or spice grinder, and grind until powdered. Transfer to the bowl of a food processor.

4. Drain the chiles, reserving the soaking liquid. Add the chiles, shrimp paste, lemongrass, ginger, garlic, and shallots to the food processor, and process until a moist paste forms. Add up to ½ cup of the soaking liquid to aid in grinding.

5. Use the paste immediately, refrigerate in an airtight container for up to 1 month, or freeze for up to 3 months.

Cooking tip: To cut down on the time making curry pastes, try to always double or triple the recipe and store a few batches for curries to enjoy another time. Place the curry paste in 1-cup portions to freeze, as most recipes call for this amount when making a large batch. Once you have a few in the freezer, creating quick-and-easy slow cooker curries is a breeze.

Jungle Curry Paste

nam prik kaeng pa

SOY-FREE | NUT-FREE   Deriving its name from the northern jungles of its origin, jungle curry is one of the few Thai curries that forgo coconut milk in their preparation. The result is a blazing hot curry, but also an herbal one, with the addition of a generous portion of Thai basil and chives.

MAKES 1 CUP
PREP TIME: 30 MINUTES

¼ cup dried cayenne chiles, stemmed and seeded

1 stalk lemongrass, outer leaves peeled and discarded, lower stalk thinly sliced

⅓ cup cilantro stems (reserve the leaves for another recipe)

¼ cup diced ginger

½ cup diced shallots

4 serrano chiles

2 Thai chiles

3 teaspoons shrimp paste

½ cup Thai basil

¼ cup sliced chives

1. In a small bowl, cover the cayenne chiles with water. Soak for 30 minutes.

2. In a food processor with a metal blade, process the lemongrass, cilantro stems, ginger, shallots, serrano chiles, Thai chiles, and shrimp paste until the mixture is combined and broken up.

3. Drain the cayenne chiles, reserving the soaking liquid. Add the chiles, Thai basil, and chives to the food processor, along with a couple tablespoons of the soaking liquid to aid in grinding. Continue to process until a moist paste is formed. Add up to a ½ cup of the soaking liquid to assist in grinding.

4. Use the paste immediately, or refrigerate in an airtight container for up to 1 month, or freeze for up to 3 months.

Cooking tip: Jungle curry is one of the hottest of all Thai dishes. If you like the flavor of this curry, but don't care for the intense heat, cut back on the Thai chiles, or eliminate them altogether for a milder rendition of the classic curry.

REFERENCES

Ricker, Andy. *Pok Pok*. Berkeley: 10 Speed Press, 2013.

Sodsook, Victor. *True Thai*. New York: William Morrow and Company, Inc., 1995.

Thai Kitchen. Accessed March 2, 2015. http://www.thaikitchen.com /Recipes.aspx.

Wood, Rebecca. *The New Whole Foods Encyclopedia*. New York: Penguin Books, 2010.

RESOURCES

Online resources for Thai food products:

eFoodDepot
http://www.efooddepot.com/ethnics/thai.html

Grocery Thai
http://grocerythai.com/

Import Food
importfood.com.

Taste Pad Thai
http://www.tastepadthai.com/

Temple of Thai
http://www.templeofthai.com/food/

CONVERSION TABLES

....

VOLUME EQUIVALENTS (LIQUID)

US STANDARD	US STANDARD (OUNCES)	METRIC (APPROXIMATE)
2 tablespoons	1 fl. oz.	30 mL
¼ cup	2 fl. oz.	60 mL
½ cup	4 fl. oz.	120 mL
1 cup	8 fl. oz.	240 mL
1½ cups	12 fl. oz.	355 mL
2 cups or 1 pint	16 fl. oz.	475 mL
4 cups or 1 quart	32 fl. oz.	1 L
1 gallon	128 fl. oz.	4 L

OVEN TEMPERATURES

FAHRENHEIT (F)	CELSIUS (C) (APPROXIMATE)
250	120
300	150
325	165
350	180
375	190
400	200
425	220
450	230

VOLUME EQUIVALENTS (DRY)

US STANDARD	METRIC (APPROXIMATE)
⅛ teaspoon	0.5 mL
¼ teaspoon	1 mL
½ teaspoon	2 mL
¾ teaspoon	4 mL
1 teaspoon	5 mL
1 tablespoon	15 mL
¼ cup	59 mL
⅓ cup	79 mL
½ cup	118 mL
⅔ cup	156 mL
¾ cup	177 mL
1 cup	235 mL
2 cups or 1 pint	475 mL
3 cups	700 mL
4 cups or 1 quart	1 L
½ gallon	2 L
1 gallon	4 L

WEIGHT EQUIVALENTS

US STANDARD	METRIC (APPROXIMATE)
½ ounce	15 g
1 ounce	30 g
2 ounces	60 g
4 ounces	115 g
8 ounces	225 g
12 ounces	340 g
16 ounces or 1 pound	455 g

RECISE INDEX

RECIPE INDEX

INDEX

....

CPSIA information can be obtained
at www.ICGtesting.com
Printed in the USA
JSHW042029010720
6423JS00009B/136